本书为2022年浙江省教育科学规划课题（项目编号：2022SCG146）、2021年教育部第二批产学合作协同育人项目（项目编号：201102107002）和2020年衢州学院校级新形态教材建设项目（项目编号：XXTJC202004）的阶段性成果。

美英报刊文章选读
（上）

主　编　袁知乾　周子静

副主编　肖新新　钟茂彬　彭承进

上海交通大学出版社
SHANGHAI JIAO TONG UNIVERSITY PRESS

内容提要

本书主要为大学本科英语专业阅读课程编写。全书共分14章,主要包括时事新闻、商业资讯、文化传承、生活百科、体坛风云、文娱在线、教育视窗、旅途人生、科技前沿、环境保护、社会风貌等内容,注重题材广泛性和内容深刻性的有机结合。本书各单元均设有课前阅读思考题、两篇课文、生词表、课文注释,并配备题型多样、内容丰富的课后练习。书中内容皆选自原版材料,原汁原味,语言地道,可作为广大英语学习者有益的阅读素材。

图书在版编目（CIP）数据

美英报刊文章选读. 上 / 袁知乾,周子静主编. —
上海：上海交通大学出版社,2022.8
ISBN 978-7-313-26841-9

I.①美… II.①袁… ②周… III.①英语—阅读教
学—高等学校—自学参考资料 IV.①H319.4

中国版本图书馆CIP数据核字（2022）第084701号

美英报刊文章选读（上）

MEIYING BAOKAN WENZHANG XUANDU (SHANG)

主　　编	袁知乾　周子静		地　　址	上海市番禺路951号
出版发行	上海交通大学出版社		电　　话	021-64071208
邮政编码	200030		经　　销	全国新华书店
印　　制	上海天地海设计印刷有限公司		印　　张	12.5
开　　本	787 mm × 1092 mm　1/16			
字　　数	289千字			
版　　次	2022年8月第1版		印　　次	2022年8月第1次印刷
书　　号	ISBN 978-7-313-26841-9		电子书号	ISBN 978-7-89424-290-7
定　　价	49.00元			

在当今全球化高速发展的时代,世事瞬息万变。要了解国内外发展变化的动态,就需要阅读大量的材料,特别是及时反映当前时事资讯的报刊杂志和网络文章。从语言学习的角度来说,阅读是学好一门语言的最佳途径。对于外语学习者来说,听、说、读、写、译中的"读"始终占据着不可替代的位置。教育部在《高等学校英语专业本科教学质量国家标准》中强调对英语专业人才的培养要"突出人文素质教育,注重开阔学生的国际视野",要"了解英语国家的历史和当代社会的政治、经济、文化、科技、军事等基本情况",要"突出语言综合运用能力和思辨能力的培养"。毫无疑问,阅读是达到以上标准的必要途径。

当今信息化时代,报刊(含网络电子报刊)的重要性也日益突出。在多年的阅读教学实践中,作者也发现阅读英语报刊是提高学生阅读能力、形成良好阅读习惯的有效途径。报刊的内容本身包罗万象,涵盖政治、经济、文化、社会、体育、卫生等诸多领域。阅读报刊不仅仅可以帮助学生增加英语词汇量,帮助他们记忆、理解、巩固所学的词汇、语法等语言知识,还可以提高他们对各专业、各行业的认知水平,拓宽知识面,开阔国际视野。此外,英语报刊阅读对于英语学习者的语言知识产出也有着无可替代的作用。古语有云:"读万卷书,行万里路""熟读唐诗三百首,不会吟诗也会吟",讲的就是这个道理。美国著名语言教育家斯蒂芬·克拉申(Stephen D. Krashen)认为"阅读是成功习得第二语言的最佳路径"(People acquiring a second language have the best chance for success through reading)。

本书正是基于以上时代背景和教育理念而编写的。全书共14章,内容涉及时事新闻、商业资讯、文化传承、生活百科、体坛风云、文娱在线、教育视窗、旅途人生、科技前沿、环境保护、社会风貌等各领域,注重题材广泛性和内容深刻性的结合。本书各单元均设有课前阅读思考题、两篇课文、生词表、专业术语注释和课后练习。其中,课后练习针对性强、题型多样,兼顾知识巩固和视野拓展的效果,各单元课后都配有一篇与本单元主题相关的完形填空的文章。书中内容皆选自英美各大知名报刊的原版材料,经过编者精心甄选,语言地道,内容丰富,视角新颖,因此对于英语学习者的阅读能力和其他语言能力的提升颇有帮助。

本书主要为大学英语本科专业学生设计和编写的,也可以作为公共英语的拓展课程教材,对于广大英语爱好者来说也是一本非常有益的英语自学读物。

本书由袁知乾进行总体设计、组织编写和统稿,周子静为共同主编,肖新新、钟茂彬和彭承进为副主编。作者编写分工如下:袁知乾负责编写前言、第1、2、3、4、14单元;周子静负责编写第5、6、7、8单元;肖新新负责编写第9、10、11单元;钟茂彬负责编写第12、13单元;彭承进协助统稿、审稿。

在本书编写过程中,我们参阅借鉴了大量有关英语阅读方面的前沿书刊资料,并得到了有关专家、教授的悉心指导,在此一并致谢。因编者水平局限,本书难免存在疏漏和不足之处,望各位专家和读者批评指正。

编　者

目　录
Contents

Unit 1 Business

Part I Pre-reading Questions

1. What is the impact of COVID-19 pandemic on the business?
2. How does the COVID-19 pandemic change consumer behaviors?
3. What kind of companies need be transformed in the age full of fierce competition?
4. What are the common features of successful businesses?

Part II Intensive Reading

Text A

Interconnected Economy: Is Your Business at Risk?

Though often uncomfortable, change is necessary. There are situations in which we cannot control all the factors that affect the way we interact and the way we do business. The coronavirus crisis is a case in point: It is mercilessly exposing weaknesses and forcing change while showing us how interconnected the economy is — and how much more connected it needs to become.

According to management consultancy Roland Berger, businesses that invest in digital innovations today will be better prepared for the future and, as a result, be able to respond more flexibly to changes. To make that happen, companies must turn any momentum resulting from the pandemic to their advantage.

Technologies like artificial intelligence and machine learning provide momentum, offer opportunities, and open up new avenues. In short, they provide freedom and new opportunity to create business model and process innovations.

Three key trends point to what business models must deliver in the future:

Digitalization offers opportunities for companies to outshine their competitors

Product- and service-centric approaches promise greater added value for customers.

1

Increasingly, enterprises are selling not just products, but traditional and digital services too — sometimes as a package. Technical solutions are the foundation for consumption-based and subscription-based business models. Thus, a machine manufacturer will sell not only machinery or household appliances, but also services such as installation by video conference, remote configuration, predictive maintenance — or even a service instead of a product. That's not a distant vision. That's reality.

Customers are overwhelmed with information and offers

One way to capture their attention and win their loyalty is through "hyper-personalization", that is, by offering products that are tailored to their needs — from personalized sport shoes to complex, individually configured machines.

The customer experience does not end with a purchase

Packaging, shipping, and the way companies handle complaints and returns have a much greater impact on the customer experience than the purchase itself. And customer experience has a huge influence on future buying decisions. Stable, sustainable supply chains have become a unique selling point. After the purchase is before the purchase.

If they are to move with these three trends, companies need to embrace digital transformation. The technical solutions are there, but there's more to it than that. The coronavirus crisis has highlighted how fragmented and fragile linear supply and value chains can be. "Resilience" is the magic word here. It doesn't take wizardry to achieve it, but it does mean creating agile and cooperative working models for your own company and for doing business with others.

A new mindset is crucial. The idea of platform-based, cooperative approaches can be applied to the manufacturing sector, particularly to German SMEs — the backbone of the country's economy. In terms of connected value creation in the German SME industry, the German Federal Ministry for Economics refers to an alliance of machine manufacturers in the German state of Thuringia — they rent machinery to one another, are able to make better and more efficient use of their resources, and consequently, can do and achieve much more than before.

Clearly, value chains need to become value networks. Three trends describe the key characteristics of new networks.

Transparency, agility, and flexibility

An expert report on value networks in times of pandemic infection published by the German National Academy of Science and Engineering, identifies four resilience drivers: anticipation, preparation, transparency, and speed. Around 70% of the companies surveyed rated each of the following measures for mitigating the effects of potential infection crises as (very) important: close cooperation with suppliers and customers; standardized data exchange with suppliers, customers, and logistics services providers; and multiple sourcing. Value networks provide transparent insights, allowing contributors to make decisions faster and with greater agility and flexibility.

Alliances make the individual and the group stronger

Catena-X, an alliance formed in 2020, aims to create end-to-end data chains for value chain processes in the automotive industry. Manufacturers, component suppliers, and IT companies — from large enterprises to SMEs — expect the alliance to open up scope for new value-added services and make the automotive industry more competitive.

Looking ahead, it could even eliminate the need for large-scale vehicle recalls to replace defective parts, because the information would be available to offer the owners of the vehicles affected a repair shop appointment directly — rather than having to recall the entire model run. That's good for customers, and it has a positive economic effect too.

Companies need to act in a more economically and ecologically sustainable way

We have to change our behavior. To satisfy the current demand for natural resources, the Earth would need to be 1.6 times its actual size. Regulators, investors, and consumers are calling for clear action to reduce emissions and energy consumption. This in turn is putting pressure on businesses and their supply chains, whose emissions are on average more than five times higher than those of the business itself. We can't just carry on as before. Value networks help companies to operate more sustainably by enabling them to pinpoint the emissions created in the procurement, manufacture, and distribution of products.

Bottom line: Digital transformation is the cornerstone for new business models and value networks. And it provides the transparency and scope for enterprises to become more sustainable. By not confronting change, companies place their own futures at risk. But if they adopt an agile approach, they will rise to and grow with the challenges.

Total words: 949

Total Reading Time: _____ minutes _____ seconds

💬 **Vocabulary**

coronavirus *n.* 冠状病毒

momentum *n.* 冲力；推进力；动力；势头；动量

pandemic *adj.*（疾病）在全国（或世界）流行的

　　　　　n.（全国或全球性）流行病；瘟疫

outshine *v.* 比……做得好；使逊色

configuration *n.* 布局，构造；配置

fragmented *adj.* 片断的；成碎片的

resilience *n.* 快速恢复的能力；弹力；适应力

wizardry *n.* 杰出的成就；非凡的才能

agile *adj.*（动作）敏捷的；（思维）机敏的

transparent *adj.* 透明的，清澈的；易懂的

mitigate *v.* 缓和；减轻

ecologically *adv.* 从生态学的观点看

emission *n.* 排放物；（尤指光、热、气等的）发出；排放

pinpoint *v.* 明确指出，确定（位置或时间）

　　　　　n. 极小的范围，光点

procurement *n.* 采购；购买

cornerstone *n.* 基石，奠基石，基础

Phrases

automotive industry 汽车工业；汽车制造业

be overwhelmed with 被……淹没；被……压倒

value-added service 增值服务

Notes

predictive maintenance: Predictive maintenance is designed to help determine the condition of in-service equipment so as to estimate when maintenance should be performed. It is regarded as condition-based maintenance carried out as suggested by estimations of the degradation state of an item.

supply chain: A supply chain refers to a network between a company and its suppliers to produce and distribute a specific product to the final buyer. This network includes different activities, people, entities, information, and resources. The supply chain also represents the steps it takes to get the product or service from its original state to the customer.

value chain: A value chain refers to a business model that describes the full range of activities which are needed to create a product or service. For companies that produce goods, a value chain includes the steps that involve bringing a product from conception to distribution, and everything in between — such as procuring raw materials, manufacturing functions, and marketing activities.

value network: A value network is a set of connections between organizations and/or individuals interacting with each other to benefit the entire group. A value network allows members to buy and sell products as well as share information.

Exercises

I. **Answer the following questions after reading the text.**

　　1. According to the text, what do businessmen have to learn from the coronavirus crisis

in terms of doing business?

2. Why do businesses that invest in digital innovations have much more advantages in confronting changes?

3. What do value-added service mean for a machine manufacturer that promises value-added service for customers?

4. What does "hyper-personalization" mean according to the text?

5. Why does the author's statement "After the purchase is before the purchase" is not logically paradoxical?

II. Decide whether the following statements are true or false according to the text.

1. Consumption-based and subscription-based business models have not been technically realized until now.

2. Companies need to be transformed digitally in confronting the coronavirus crisis.

3. Since the coronavirus crisis has rendered linear supply and value chains fragmented and fragile, it is hardly realistic for companies to achieve resilience.

4. The case of Catena-X is employed to illustrate the fact that alliances make the individual and the group stronger and companies need to act in a more economically and ecologically sustainable way.

5. Value networks can help companies reduce emission and operate for a longer time.

III. Fill in the blank of the following sentences with one of the words given below. Change the form where necessary.

emission	transparent	fragment	procurement	agile
mitigate	pandemic	configuration	ecological	momentum

1. The forest of streamers from the wharf to the ship's rail slowly broke as the vessel gained _____ .

2. The global health _____ had caused many major sports competitions to be cancelled or postponed.

3. These discrete building blocks must have individually useful optical properties and easily integrate with other optical materials in a broad range of _____ .

4. They can use the intervening few years to make their markets more competitive, _____ more transparent and foreign investment much easier.

5. This kind of software can make any size company more efficient, more _____ , more responsive.

6. The highly _____ nature of the industry will cap the prices that operators can

charge.

7. Global warming results from the _____ of heat trapping gases, such as carbon dioxide and methane.

8. They could get bogged down in legal argument, factor in _____ circumstances and take previous behaviour into consideration.

9. Measurement and information systems need to be developed to provide full _____ throughout public education.

10. Plentiful and inexpensive, clay is also one of the most _____ clean building materials available.

IV. Translate the following sentences into Chinese.

1. The coronavirus crisis is a case in point: It is mercilessly exposing weaknesses and forcing change while showing us how interconnected the economy is — and how much more connected it needs to become.

2. Product- and service-centric approaches promise greater added value for customers. Increasingly, enterprises are selling not just products, but traditional and digital services too — sometimes as a package.

3. One way to capture their attention and win their loyalty is through "hyper-personalization", that is, by offering products that are tailored to their needs — from personalized sport shoes to complex, individually configured machines.

4. And customer experience has a huge influence on future buying decisions. Stable, sustainable supply chains have become a unique selling point.

5. By not confronting change, companies place their own futures at risk. But if they adopt an agile approach, they will rise to and grow with the challenges.

V. Select one word for each blank from the following word bank. You may not use any of the words in the bank more than once. Change the form where necessary.

agile	fragmented	collaboration	implemented	invisible
button	declines	redundant	overload	overwhelmed

Collaborative work — time spent on email, IM, phone, and video calls — has risen 50% or more over the past decade to consume 85% or more of most people's work weeks. The COVID-19 pandemic caused this figure to take another sharp upward tick, with people spending more time each week in shorter and more __1__ meetings, with voice and video call times doubling and IM traffic increasing by 65%. And to make matters worse, __2__ demands are moving further into the evening and are beginning earlier in the morning.

These demands, which can be __3__ to managers, are hurting organizations' efforts to become more __4__ and innovative. And they can lead to individual career derailment, burnout, and __5__ in physical and mental well-being.

In response, forward-looking organizations are taking action to protect employees from the *volume* of collaborative demands by employing organizational network analysis (ONA). For example:

- Two major life sciences organizations have used network analysis to systematically analyze calendar data and identify ways to reduce __6__ meeting time.

- One global software organization has focused on email to reduce volume, length, and cc'ing redundancies.

- A globally recognized insurance organization has employed network analysis to identify the most __7__ employees and educate them on practices to reduce overload.

- And, on a more dubious front, one global services organization __8__ a 60-second timeout button. After a particularly difficult time, employees can hit a __9__ that lets others know they are taking a mindfulness break. In that 60 seconds, employees practice some aspect of mindfulness — although one must wonder if this is akin to giving a band-aid to an amputee.

This exclusive focus on quantity of collaborative demands misses two important drivers of collaborative __10__ :

(1) the inefficiencies and subsequent cognitive switching costs of always-on cultures and

(2) the personal motivations that lead us all to jump into collaborative work too quickly.

Part III Extensive Reading

Text B

The Secret Behind Successful Corporate Transformations

Successful enterprise transformation has long been considered the holy grail of the corporate world — continually sought after, but difficult to grasp. More than 25 years ago, John Kotter highlighted the challenge when he made his now-famous assertion that 70% of corporate transformation efforts are doomed to fail.

Is Kotter's number accurate? And what makes a successful transformation? There have been surprisingly few studies that set out to answer these questions in a quantitative way. So last fall, our three organizations, Copperfield Advisory (Copperfield), Insider, and Revolution Insights Group (RIG) came together as a team to determine what puts some companies on the path to success.

Using a meta-analysis that crunched data on financial performance as well as corporate reputation, we found that:

(1) Transformation is even harder than we thought. Only 22% of companies in our analysis successfully transformed themselves. A 78% failure rate, compared with Kotter's asserted 70%, quantifiably affirms how tough it is to transform an organization.

(2) How companies engage their employees can be the difference between success and failure. Our findings revealed that companies that successfully transformed themselves shared a common focus on initiatives that prioritized employees, such as DE&I programs and support for women managers' careers, in addition to competitive pay and access to health care.

Defining transformation — and transformative organizations

Transformation is perhaps one of the most used and abused buzzwords in business today. Thus, an important first step in our study was defining what constitutes a transformation. In consultation with a panel of 60 executives from global companies, we defined "transformation" as a fundamental shift in the way that an organization conducts business, resulting in economic or social impact.

To find companies that fit this description, we identified a range of quantitative indicators that would signal what a company had experienced or was in the midst of a transformation. These included: increased R&D spend, restructuring cost spend, change in operating margin, mergers and acquisitions, name changes, and public announcements of transformation efforts. Using RIG's database, which includes information on 350 companies, we assembled a list of 128 global companies that had undergone transformation between 2016 and 2020.

At the outset of our research, we reviewed the existing literature on this topic. Surprisingly, we found that only one study — a 2018 report by Martin Reeves (et al.) of the Boston Consulting Group — had performed a quantitative evaluation of corporate transformation. That research focused on financial metrics — that is, total shareholder return — of more than 300 companies, and ultimately found that transforming successfully was most challenging for companies that faced deteriorating market performance.

Our study also assessed financial performance — based on revenue, stock price, and market value. But in addition, we added positive reputation as a criterion for success, using it as a proxy for evaluating the extent to which companies brought *all* of their stakeholders (not just shareholders) along on their transformation journeys. For this component, we used RIG's proprietary meta-equity score, which aggregates metrics from the most used and trusted rankings, including RepTrak, BrandZ, Barron's, Harris's Reputation Quotient, and Fortune's Most Admired. Through statistical analysis, we ranked the companies according to their financial and reputational performances.

What successful transformations have in common

Our assessment found that only 28 of the 128 companies we examined (i.e., 22%) successfully transformed from both financial and reputational perspectives.

Our next step was to take a closer look at these 28 organizations to identify the attributes that set them apart from the rest. Here we took inspiration from perhaps a surprising source — evolutionary biology.

In looking at the 128 companies that had undergone transformations, we identified 66 corporate attributes measuring everything from innovation and energy efficiency to customer guarantees and market depth — giving us a snapshot of how each organization dealt with customers, employees, shareholders, and its own environmental impact.

But when we looked more closely at the 28 most successful transformers, we identified 6 attributes — most of which are related to employee compensation and DE&I — that set them apart from the rest of the pack:

- Employee Pay: These employees

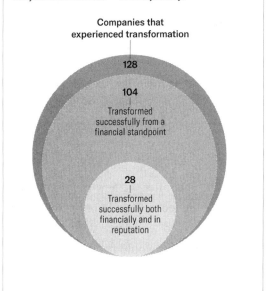

Corporate Transformation Is Harder Than We Think

Researchers identified 128 companies that underwent some degree of transformation between 2016 and 2020. But only 28 achieved both financial transformation (as measured by revenue, stock price, and market value) and reputational transformation, indicating that they brought all of their stakeholders — not just shareholders — on the journey.

Companies that experienced transformation

128

104
Transformed successfully from a financial standpoint

28
Transformed successfully both financially and in reputation

were compensated more highly compared to those at companies of a similar size.

● Employee Stock Options: Employees at these companies receive more stock options compared to those at companies of a similar size.

● Employee Satisfaction: Employees at these companies report higher satisfaction at work.

● Diversity and Inclusivity: These companies employ hiring practices with an eye toward equity.

● Women Managers: These companies employ more women in managerial positions.

● Women Employees: Women make up a higher share of employees at these companies.

We spoke to executives at one of the successful transformers to understand their keys to achieving both reputational and financial successes.

Microsoft: Unifying employees around an inclusive vision

Microsoft is one of the best-known examples of corporate transformation in recent years, moving from a software company to a cloud-services company and gaining $1.5 trillion in market capitalization. A core element of its overall restructuring and strategic shift was an overhaul of the company's vision, which in turn affected all aspects of the employee experience, from team dynamics to compensation.

In 2014, when the company began its transformation initiative, it also set out to change its corporate culture, which had previously been characterized by individualism, competitiveness, and a "know it all" attitude among employees. CEO Satya Nadella and other executives partnered with HR leaders to craft a refreshed mission and vision that better reflected the ideals of empathy, humanity, understanding of cultural differences, and Microsoft's place in the world. The result was a mission that shifted from a product focus to a more inclusive, people focus — an aim to "empower every person and organization on the planet to achieve more".

Rolling out this people-centric mission meant a lot of repetition and reinforcement. The new language was printed on office items, like company badges and coffee cups, and discussed at town hall meetings and smaller team gatherings. Compensation schemes were also revised to account for — and incentivize — teamwork and collaboration. While Microsoft's cultural transformation remains ongoing, the company tracks its success via an annual employee poll, which consistently receives an 85% response rate across the organization. It saw an uptick in results related to how employees feel about the company culture one year after the new mission was introduced. Microsoft's commitment to a growth mindset, using technology to put people first, and to leading with empathy and respect, have led to an engaged workforce where 95% of employees feel proud to work at Microsoft and 92% of employees would recommend Microsoft as a great place to work. The company also saw a 14% stock increase in that first year following the mission's roll out, between 2014 and 2015.

People are the catalysts of successful transformation

The implications of our findings are clear: Companies have a better chance at success if they focus on their people during transformation.

What's more, the *type* of employee engagement made the difference between top-tier performance and not. Companies that prioritized attributes that are fundamentally related to employee engagement, such as diversity and inclusion, in addition to traditional benefits, such as compensation or health care, saw stronger reputations and greater financial returns than other organizations. The firms that listened with intention to their employees and matched their company engagement accordingly achieved transformational success.

Total words: 1,263

Total Reading Time: _____ minutes _____ seconds

Vocabulary

assertion *n.* 明确肯定断言,声称;主张

doom *v.* 使……注定失败(或遭殃,死亡等)

　　　n. 厄运,劫数

meta-analysis *n.* 元分析

crunch *v.* 压碎;(用计算器或电脑)运算,(用计算机)捣弄、处理信息

　　　n. 困境;症结

quantifiably *adv.* 可量化地

affirm *v.* 肯定属实;申明;断言

prioritize *v.* 按重要性排列划分优先顺序;优先处理

buzzword *n.* 流行话

assemble *v.* 集合,聚集;收集;装配

deteriorate *v.* 变坏;恶化;退化

proxy *n.* 代理人;代理权;(测算用的)代替物

proprietary *adj.* 专卖的,专营的;所有权的

aggregate *v.* 总计;合计

　　　adj. 总数的;总计的

snapshot *n.* 快照;简介;简要说明

inclusivity *n.* 包容性

managerial *adj.* 经理的;管理的

overhaul *n.* 大修,检修;改造

　　　v. 彻底检修;赶上,超过

craft *n.* 工艺,手艺;船;飞行器

　　　v.(尤指用手工)精心制作

badge *n.* 徽章；证章；标记
incentivize *v.* 激励（某人做某事）
uptick *n.* 小幅增加
mindset *n.* 观念模式,思维倾向
catalyst *n.* 催化剂
top-tier *adj.* 质量最好的,顶尖的

 Phrases

a panel of 一组
at the outset of 在……开始的时候
financial metrics 财务指标
roll out 将……轧平；正式推出（新产品,服务等）

Notes

holy grail: The Holy Grail is a treasure that serves as an important motif in Arthurian literature. Different traditions describe it as a cup, dish or stone with miraculous powers that offer eternal youth or sustenance in infinite abundance, often in the custody of the Fisher King. The term "holy grail" is often used to denote an elusive object or goal that is sought after because of its great significance.

mergers and acquisitions: Mergers and acquisitions (M&A) is a general term that is uesed to describe the consolidation of companies or assets through varieties of financial transactions, including mergers, acquisitions, consolidations, tender offers, purchase of assets, and management acquisitions.

Exercises

I. **Answer the following questions after reading the text.**

1. Why did the three organizations, Copperfield Advisory (Copperfield), Insider, and Revolution Insights Group (RIG) do the research?

2. According to the three organizations' research, what is the key factor on the path to successful transformation for companies?

3. What is transformation according to the text?

4. What is the difference between the 28 most successful transformers and the rest in terms of recruiting female employees?

5. What can we learn from the corporate transformation of Microsoft?

II. Decide whether the following statements are true or false according to the text.

1. The research of Copperfield Advisory (Copperfield), Insider, and Revolution Insights Group (RIG) proved that Kotter's assertion is absolutely accurate.

2. Successfully transformed companies offer competitive pay and health care and zero in on initiatives that prioritized employees.

3. According to the text, we can learn that many scholars and organizations had performed a quantitative evaluation of corporate transformation in the past.

4. From the text we can learn that Microsoft is a typical case of successful transformers.

5. On the basis of the three organizations' reseach, the better benefits the companies offer, the more likely it will be for them to be transformed successfully.

III. Fill in the blanks with the words given in the brackets. Change the form where necessary.

1. She confidently _____ (assertion) that the videos are not faked, and that the vocal range is too broad to be made by a human.

2. The workers held out for five days, but they were _____ (doom) to defeat.

3. Their model _____ (crunch) the information under various scenarios of climate change to predict the ranges of the species in 2050.

4. They all _____ (affirm) that policies were to be judged by their contribution to social justice.

5. Those different roles must be _____ (prioritize) in their order of importance in our life.

6. If bond prices rise rapidly, it could imply that experts reckon economic conditions are _____ (deteriorate).

7. Yet _____ (aggregate) the collective wisdom and putting a probability on it is a very valuable function in itself.

8. Some prices are _____ (inclusively) of three meals, activities and entertainment.

9. It is argued that there are more men in higher _____ (manager) and executive positions than women.

10. There are a variety of methods of professional interrogation, of ways to persuade people, _____ (incentivize) people, motivate people.

IV. Translate the following sentences into Chinese.

1. Successful enterprise transformation has long been considered the holy grail of the corporate world — continually sought after, but difficult to grasp.

2. How companies engage their employees can be the difference between success and failure.

3. In consultation with a panel of 60 executives from global companies, we defined "transformation" as a fundamental shift in the way that an organization conducts business, resulting in economic or social impact.

4. The result was a mission that shifted from a product focus to a more inclusive, people focus — an aim to "empower every person and organization on the planet to achieve more".

5. Companies that prioritized attributes that are fundamentally related to employee engagement, such as diversity and inclusion, in addition to traditional benefits, such as compensation or health care, saw stronger reputations and greater financial returns than other organizations.

V. Topics for discussion.

1. What is the significance of enterprise transformation?
2. Please list some cases of successful enterprise transformation in China and try to find out their common focous.

2 Culture

Pre-reading Questions

1. What's the difference between culture and nature?
2. What do you think of the English proverb "A leopard can't change its spots"?
3. How should we treat culture conflicts in the process of communication?
4. How important is culture for a nation?

Part II **Intensive Reading**

Text A

Why It's Harder to Change Culture than Nature

One reason for our relentless "culture wars" and anxieties about "cancel culture" might be our misguided sense of what culture is — and how easily we can change it.

We used to frame everything in terms of "nature versus nurture". Either something was hard-wired and biological — such as intelligence or athletic ability — or it was cultural. The implications were always pretty clear: If anything isn't natural, it must be merely cultural.

If something was mappable in our genes or identifiable with multicolored brain scans, it was deemed real and difficult to change. Maybe even impossible. And moral arguments weren't too far behind. If God designed things a certain way, how dare we tamper with them?

Of course, much of our thinking about human life has long pivoted on the search for biological answers to social questions. From gene splicing to mRNA vaccines, we have gotten better and better at deciphering some of nature's most complex secrets to suit our goals.

Operation Warp Speed is a large-scale example of just how efficient we've become at bending biology and science to fit our needs: in this instance, creating a vaccine in record-breaking time as we attempt to beat back a global pandemic. However, that very same pandemic shows us how much less effective we are at the cultural side of the ledger.

Just because science was able to tee up a vaccine faster than ever before doesn't mean that we are anywhere near as adept at dealing with the intractably cultural reasons why so many people are skeptical about taking it. The same skepticism seems to have caused five governors to roll back their states' mask mandates, despite urgent warnings from public health officials.

What science makes possible, cultural impulses can overturn. We see this in conspiracy theories likening the vaccine to a global Trojan horse, a concerted effort to harm the entire world's population while pretending to heal it (And that is not even the most bizarre conspiracy theory getting debunked or defended on cable news programs these days).

If culture is, as anthropologists like me describe it, everything that we have to learn while living together in the world, what counts as "culture" is stunningly ubiquitous and undeniably comprehensive.

When I want students to think about the inescapability of culture, I usually start by asking them to tell me what is not culture, what they didn't have to learn how to do or use or love or believe in. They usually come up with answers such as breathing and going to the bathroom   though even the latter is complicated by the rules we internalize from society about how, where, when and with whom we can go, especially in public (Think of the controversies over which public restrooms transgender people should use).

As we continue to improve our mastery of nature, it's very often at the expense of appreciating the harder nut to crack that cultural practices and beliefs represent. We look for laws of culture, but they aren't nearly as easy to identify or rely on as the laws of science.

Why does that matter? And what can we do about it? First, we need to recognize that there is nothing mere about culture. Not at all. In the nature-versus-nurture debates we will continue to have in the 21st century, it is nature that will increasingly seem more predictably receptive to our demands, ever more susceptible to our scientific breakthroughs. In the future, we could start to think of things as merely biological.

Even with something like climate change, the science of how to tackle it seems fairly clear. It's our cultural commitment that's lacking. So while we may get better at predicting, measuring and potentially counteracting natural events, culture will continue to confound us.

We should not keep making the mistake of believing that science can solve our most pressing social dilemmas. There isn't a pill we can pop to eliminate cultural conflicts. And if there were, we would be wise not to take it. The better treatment is a lifelong willingness to listen to and learn from other people in ways that might help to humble the worst forms of hubris about our own cultural claims.

Culture changes slowly, often unpredictably. While so-called cancel culture might pounce on people in an instant, our continuing wars over cultural ideals and beliefs are much more like drawn-out, self-destructive battles of mutual attrition. And if we continue to wage them as we do, all of us could actually lose.

Total words: 849

Total Reading Time: _____ minutes _____ seconds

Vocabulary

relentless *adj.* 不停的；持续强烈的；严格的；苛刻的；无情的

misguided *adj.* 被误导的；（因理解或判断失误）搞错的

hard-wired *adj.* 硬（布）线的；（计算机）硬接线的

mappable *adj.* 使（基因）在染色体上定位的

tamper *v.* 篡改；擅自改动；胡乱摆弄

pivot *n.* 枢轴；中心点；中心

　　　v. （使）在枢轴上转动

decipher *v.* 破解；辨认

ledger *n.* （会计）分类账簿

intractably *adv.* 很难对付（或处理）地

skeptical *adj.* 怀疑的，持怀疑态度的

skepticism *n.* 怀疑态度；怀疑主义

mandate *n.* 授权，委托书；（政府的）任期

overturn *v.* 推翻

conspiracy *n.* 合谋，密谋

liken *v.* 把……比作

bizarre *adj.* 极其怪诞的；异乎寻常的

debunk *v.* 批判；驳斥；揭穿……的真相

anthropologist *n.* 人类学家

stunningly *adv.* 绝妙地；令人震惊地

ubiquitous *adj.* 似乎无所不在的；十分普遍的

inescapability *n.* 不可避免性

thwart *v.* 阻止；阻挠；对……构成阻力

destructive *adj.* 破坏性的，毁灭性的

hell-bent *adj.* 不顾一切地（做某事）

receptive *adj.* （对新观点、建议等）愿意倾听的，乐于接受的

susceptible *adj.* 易受影响的；敏感，感情丰富的

counteract *v.* 抵制；抵消

confound *v.* 使困惑惊讶，使惊疑；证明……有错；击败

pressing *adj.* 紧迫的

humble *adj.* 谦逊的；虚心的；（级别或地位）低下的

　　　v. 贬低，使感到卑微；轻松打败（尤指强大的对手）

hubris *n.* 傲慢；狂妄

pounce *v.* 突袭；猛扑

drawn-out *adj.* 延长的；拖延的

attrition *n.*（尤指对敌人造成的）削弱，消耗

wage *n.* 工资，报酬

　　　v. 进行，发动（战争，战斗等）

Phrases

tamper with 篡改

pivot on 围绕（主旨）；以……为核心

gene splicing 基因拼接；基因剪接；基因接合

tee up 置（球）于球座上；准备；安排

roll back 击退；削减

pounce on 抓住机会（以便批评）

Notes

cancel culture: Cancel culture refers to the popular practice of withdrawing (canceling) support for public figures and companies after they have done or said something considered objectionable or offensive. It is generally discussed as being performed on social media in the form of group shaming.

gene splicing: Gene splicing refers to a process employing recombinant DNA technology to join, by attachment or insertion, a DNA segment from one source to a DNA segment from another source.

Operation Warp Speed: Operation Warp Speed (OWS) was created in America in May 2020. It served as a partnership between the Departments of Health and Human Services (HHS) and Defense (DOD), aiming to help accelerate the development of a COVID-19 vaccine.

Trojan horse: The Trojan horse was the wooden horse used by the Greeks, during the Trojan War, to enter the city of Troy and win the war. Metaphorically, a "Trojan horse" has come to mean any trick or stratagem that causes a target to invite a foe into a securely protected bastion or place.

checkerboard pattern: Also known as a "checkered pattern" or simply "checksx", a checkerboard pattern is a black and white graphic resembling a checkerboard that often adorns articles of clothing, particularly footwear, handbags, and smaller accessories such as wristbands, pins, and wallets.

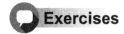 **Exercises**

I. **Answer the following questions after reading the text.**

1. According to the author, what problems have our human beings focused on for a long time with regard to human life?

2. Why does the author mention Operation Warp Speed?

3. What does the author want to illustrate by saying that so many people are skeptical about taking vaccines?

4. Why is it harder to change culture than nature?

5. What advice does the author give on coping with cultural conflict?

II. **Decide whether the following statements are true or false according to the text.**

1. We used to treat the relationship between nature and nurture from the perspective of a binary opposition.

2. According to the author's points of view, we can't change the things designed by the creator.

3. Scientific problems can be solved much more effectively than ever before, so can cultural ones.

4. The author argues that anthropologists take a positive attitude towards culture.

5. According to the text, there must be an effective solution to dealing with the issue of cultural conflicts.

III. **Fill in the blank of the following sentences with one of the words or phrases given below. Change the form where necessary.**

skepticism	tamper	press	conspiracy	relentless
destroy	pivot	debunk	misguide	liken

1. The metaphor that _____ the brain to a computer is misleading and in another discussion somewhere, sometime, I will tell you why that is.

2. The spirited debate about online education _____ on the technological achievements of the past decade.

3. Except this was not war, there were no other _____ issues that demanded his immediate attention so he could forget his pain.

4. More importantly, it _____ the idea that educational reform is instituted to enhance the skills of the labour force.

5. The problem with _____ theories is that they give people who spot real

conspiracies a bad name.

6. But there's a massive machine already in place that produces representations of our community that are often _____, sometimes hateful.

7. They might gain access to our systems and _____ with data through computer network attacks or exploit it for hostile purposes.

8. Alcohol is as _____ to health worldwide as smoking and high blood pressure, it was claimed today.

9. Although most respondents were enthusiastic or supportive of booking, about a quarter were _____ or not convinced of its value.

10. Smoke covered the neighborhood where intense gunfire was _____.

IV. Translate the following sentences into Chinese.

1. We used to frame everything in terms of "nature versus nurture". Either something was hard-wired and biological — such as intelligence or athletic ability — or it was cultural.

2. The same skepticism seems to have caused five governors to roll back their states' mask mandates, despite urgent warnings from public health officials.

3. If culture is, as anthropologists like me describe it, everything that we have to learn while living together in the world, what counts as "culture" is stunningly ubiquitous and undeniably comprehensive.

4. In the nature-versus-nurture debates we will continue to have in the 21st century, it is nature that will increasingly seem more predictably receptive to our demands, ever more susceptible to our scientific breakthroughs.

5. So while we may get better at predicting, measuring and potentially counteracting natural events, culture will continue to confound us.

V. Select one word for each blank from the following word bank. You may not use any of the words in the bank more than once. Change the form where necessary.

| benefit | accountability | balance | cultivate | validity |
| career | effective | revoke | opposite | problematic |

The effectiveness of cancel culture remains in debate as Gen Z grapples with the best response for holding influencers and celebrities accountable.

Cancel culture is the mass withdrawal of public support for a celebrity or public figure — typically after the person says or does something that the public may deem as __1__. The act of "cancelling" has become a hot topic of debate among Gen Z as they argue the __2__ of the practice.

If at its core it accomplishes the set goal of holding those in the public eye accountable for the insensitive things they may say or do, it is a quick way to end a person's __3__ before it can even begin. The debate over the capabilities of cancel culture has prompted the opinions of people far and wide.

Natia Fears, a senior health science major, doesn't believe the effectiveness of cancel culture.

"I don't think that cancel culture is an __4__ long-term solution for an artist," Fears said.

She said she feels that the power of cancel culture is unfairly __5__ across the board.

"It doesn't work the same way for every celebrity," Fears said. "Sometimes it works and produces a genuine change, but sometimes it just ends their career."

According to Fears, cancel culture has its __6__ : it opens a conversation for the problematic behavior to be addressed and makes space to have difficult conversations about hard topics.

Ellie Lehto, a sophomore ASL major, says the public often evokes the rite of cancel culture too quickly instead of demanding accountability, and there is a major difference between __7__ and cancel culture.

She says cancel culture is a warped version of accountability.

"Accountability breaches into cancel culture when the person's 'I'm sorry' is ignored," Lehto said.

Lehto says cancel culture often __8__ the humanity of artists as it does not give them a chance to apologize and learn from their behavior and reduces them to their mistakes.

Instead of fostering an environment that allows for education and growth, it does the __9__. It champions a one-strike rule that requires immediate apology to placate the public.

Lehto says that she believes accountability is the only way to cultivate true change and she says that you can't do that through cancel culture.

Some people believe cancel culture is effective at __10__ a culture of education, awareness, and sensitivity to our behavior and language; however, there are people who worry that cancel culture is not an effective replacement for accountability.

Part III Extensive Reading

Text B

Why Art and Culture Is Good for the Soul, the West End and the UK

As central London begins to unlock and open up, it is vital we play up to the great strengths it displays in normal times, as the heart of an interconnected ecosystem of world-class attractions, which together add up to much more than the sum of their parts.

London's retail, hospitality and cultural sectors depend on and feed off each other, and like any rare and precious ecosystem, their success and survival is inextricably linked.

During the first lockdown in March 2020, the Heart of London Business Alliance commissioned urban consultants Arup to assess how the arts and cultural sector would fare between then and 2024 under various scenarios.

Under the worst-case scenario, where London experienced repeated lockdowns, there would be a catastrophic 97% decrease in economic output, which would amount to a total loss of £18.5 billion in GVA — the value of goods and services — in the period from 2020 to 2024.

At times over the past year, this worst-case scenario looked set to become reality. With a second lockdown swiftly followed by the long third winter lockdown, the extinction of the sector in one of the most culturally rich areas in the world looked like a real possibility.

Now, though, as more and more theatres and galleries reopen their doors, there is every chance that the cycle of lockdowns has been broken at last and the sector is finally beginning to make its comeback.

The importance of art and culture cannot be underestimated

Nobody truly knows what the future holds and how society's priorities have changed over the past year. What we do know is that the importance of art and culture cannot be underestimated. Throughout this crisis, the whole nation has craved inspiration, creativity and solace, all of which is to be found inside our institutions' walls.

It is revealing how many businesses in the West End struggled to attract people back during the first unlockings, notwithstanding the various restrictions, because cultural institutions and theatres were not permitted to open, meaning that the draw was not there.

That realization has led to a renewed appreciation of the importance of the value of art and culture.

For instance, the arts and culture have a vital role in the real estate sphere, whether that's businesses trying to get their staff back into offices or investors seeking to futureproof their assets by making them universally attractive.

But this phenomenon has little to do with once more enjoying unfettered access to the arts and performances in the West End's great institutions and venues. It is more to do with creating an environment in the West End in which people can do as much as they like, and see creativity easily and for free, perhaps without even realizing it.

Let's take to the streets!

Part of this changing West End experience is the idea of bringing culture onto the streets and integrating art into the built environment. This is part of Heart of London's long-term strategy, to reset the relationship between businesses, members of the public and local cultural institutions.

Heart of London has been doing this for a while, with its Scenes in the Square, the outdoor sculpture trail of movie and TV characters dotted around Leicester Square. It features entertainment icons from the past 100 years, including firm favourites Harry Potter, Laurel and Hardy, Bugs Bunny, Gene Kelly in *Singin' in the Rain*, Mary Poppins, Mr. Bean, Paddington and DC Superheroes Batman and Wonder Woman.

They have now launched Art of London, which brings art out beyond the walls of our cultural institutions using augmented reality to create a "gallery without walls". The Art of London Augmented Gallery, which launched in May, is a unique collaboration between the Royal Academy of Arts, the National Gallery, the National Portrait Gallery and Sky Arts. The open-air gallery consists of 20 life-size colourful frames and plaques on walls around the West End, each of which contain QR codes and unique markers to unlock timeless masterpieces framed in 3D.

These are examples of a world-class cultural district stepping up in the fight to survive and thrive this year, and which is innovating to improve the public's experience when visiting the West End, offering new ways to absorb its rich culture as pandemic conditions recede.

The West End's streets also need reframing

It will be more important than ever to have spaces in the West End that people want to come back to, particularly as footfall from workers and tourists picks up. Some people will understandably need extra encouragement and will expect an improved and different experience in the capital's cultural heartland.

Westminster City Council has already begun efforts to recreate a buzz in the capital through the eye-catching Marble Arch Mound, a 25-metre-high grassy hill rising over the rooftops at the entrance to Oxford Street. In all, £150 million is being spent on Oxford Street and its surrounding area, and ￡25 million is being spent on Aldwych as well.

Now it is crucial that public funding is used to bolster other key areas of the West End to boost their revival — because when Central London is thriving, the benefits are enormous for the whole of the UK as well.

It is incredible to think that just a stone's throw away from Leicester Square and Piccadilly Circus are some of the quietest streets in Central London — such as Panton Street and the service streets off Trafalgar Square and Haymarket.

These could flourish as a new Arts Quarter, with inclusive gallery spaces, and be reinvented in the same way as Heddon Street off Regent Street and Kingly Court off Carnaby Street.

The Heart of London Business Alliance has commissioned bold proposals to do just that, which include widening footways, creating a new public space outside the National Gallery and designing out crime in the area by installing better lighting and sight lines.

When London succeeds, so does the rest of the UK

After its long hibernation, now is the time to reinvigorate the West End. London's unlocking is a tremendous opportunity to make lasting improvements — and what is most important of all is that the different parts of Central London's magical ecosystem seamlessly overlap.

Emotionally as well as economically, the cultural sector is such a key part of London, not only an asset to the local and national economy but also representative of Britain's standing in the world, and comprising the very heart and soul of the nation.

Total words: 1,124

Total Reading Time: _____ minutes _____ seconds

🗨 Vocabulary

inextricably *adv.* 不可分开地，密不可分地

lockdown *n.* 活动限制，行动限制

scenario *n.* 设想，方案；（电影或戏剧的）剧情梗概

worst-case *adj.* 最坏情况的

catastrophic *adj.* 灾难性的

underestimate *v.* 低估

crave *v.* 渴望；恳求

solace *n.* 安慰；慰藉

notwithstanding *prep.* 虽然，尽管
          adv. 尽管如此

futureproof *v.* 使不过时
       adj. 不会过时的

unfettered *adj.* 无限制的；不受约束的；自由的

dot *n.* 点，小圆点

   v. 加点；遍布于；布满，点缀

plaque *n.* (纪念性的) 牌匾

footfall *n.* 脚步声；(商店等的) 客流量

heartland *n.* (国家或地区的) 腹地；中心区域

buzz *n.* 嗡嗡声，蜂鸣声；(愉快、兴奋或成就的) 强烈情感

bolster *v.* 改善；加强

hibernation *n.* 冬眠

reinvigorate *v.* 使再振作

seamlessly *adv.* 无缝地

Phrases

feed off 以……为食；从……中得到滋养

a stone's throw 一步之遥，咫尺

Notes

the West End: The West End, commonly referred to as the West End of London, is a district of Central London, west of the City of London and north of the River Thames, in which many of the city's major tourist attractions, shops, businesses, government buildings and entertainment venues, including West End theatres, are concentrated.

Scenes in the Square: Scenes in the Square is a film-themed sculpture trail in Leicester Square, London. Eight sculptures, which were installed in February 2020, depict characters from the last 100 years of cinema including Laurel and Hardy, Mary Poppins, Batman, Bugs Bunny, Don Lockwood, Paddington Bear, Mr. Bean, and Wonder Woman. A sculpture of Harry Potter was installed later on in 2020, and then in 2021, a sculpture of the Iron Throne from *Game of Thrones* was added.

circadian rhythm: Circadian rhythm, as part of the body's internal clock, refers to 24-hour cycles. It runs in the background to carry out essential functions. One of the most important and well-known circadian rhythms is the sleep-wake cycle.

sleep hygiene: Sleep hygiene refers to science-backed practices — during the day and before bedtime — that help create thd ideal conditions for healthy sleep. It can mean the difference between a restful night and a restless one.

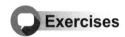 **Exercises**

I. Answer the following questions after reading the text.

1. What does "the sector" refer to in the statement "... the extinction of the sector in one of the most culturally rich areas in the world looked like a real possibility"?

2. What's the relationship between culture sectors and business sectors?

3. What does the author try to convey by citing the case of the real estate sphere?

4. What's the purpose for bringing culture onto the streets and integrating art into the built environment?

5. Why will the rest of the UK succeed when London succeeds?

II. Decide whether the following statements are true or false according to the text.

1. From the text, we can learn that London suffered a heavy economical loss in 2020.

2. The art and culture sector wasn't revived eventually.

3. Scenes in the Square only served to entertain the public.

4. The development of Central London is vital to the whole of the UK.

5. The author felt pessimistic about the future of the art and culture sector in London.

III. Fill in the blanks with the words given in the brackets. Change the form where necessary.

1. What's missing are the historical contexts of our mixing of cultures and technologies, and how _____ (inextricably) they have always been from relations of power.

2. Had it been accepted they would have had a local environmental _____ (catastrophic) and a national commercial disaster.

3. The last six years, the local government has been grossly _____ (underestimate) its revenue, steadily.

4. He drives himself towards real danger, _____ (crave) it and seeking it out whatever the cost, but is all the time consumed by feelings of self-hate and worthlessness.

5. This method allows you to _____ (futureproof) your applications.

6. The act released its physical energies without _____ (unfetter) its will.

7. This can be seen in the more than 100 villas _____ (dot) the area, mostly built in a European style.

8. It is so easy to go out and play when you are relaxed and when you have a manager who _____ (bolster) your confidence like that.

9. The officials are fully committed to _____ (reinvigorate) the economy of the area.

10. More funds wouldn't remove those obstacles to _____ (seamlessly) service, nor would improved logistics.

IV. Translate the following sentences into Chinese.

1. London's retail, hospitality and cultural sectors depend on and feed off each other, and like any rare and precious ecosystem, their success and survival is inextricably linked.

2. Now, though, as more and more theatres and galleries reopen their doors, there is every chance that the cycle of lockdowns has been broken at last and the sector is finally beginning to make its comeback.

3. Throughout this crisis, the whole nation has craved inspiration, creativity and solace, all of which is to be found inside our institutions' walls.

4. It is more to do with creating an environment in the West End in which people can do as much as they like, and see creativity easily and for free, perhaps without even realizing it.

5. Emotionally as well as economically, the cultural sector is such a key part of London, not only an asset to the local and national economy but also representative of Britain's standing in the world, and comprising the very heart and soul of the nation.

V. Topics for discussion.

1. Do you agree that the importance of art and culture cannot be underestimated? And why?

2. From your point of view, how should we develop the Chinese cultural sector amid the pandemic crisis?

Unit ③ Health

Part I Pre-reading Questions

1. What health problems will spending too much time on looking at phones cause for today's young people ?
2. Do you think texting is helpful for your daily life? Please state your points.
3. Do you have any problems of sleep phase disorder?
4. Have you experienced insomnia before? Please give some advice on solving this problem.

Part II Intensive Reading

Text A

How Texting Could Improve Your Health

In the 1970s, doctors hailed the telephone as "having become as much a part of standard medical equipment as the stethoscope". During COVID-19, the government warned the nation, via text message, to "stay at home, to protect the NHS and save lives". Used to educate and motivate, to remind and to record, mobile telephones are making inroads into health care.

Harnessing the power of phones

There are more than 8 billion mobile phone subscriptions worldwide; 8 trillion text messages are sent every year.

"Words are, of course, the most powerful drug used by mankind," said poet and novelist Rudyard Kipling in a speech to the Royal College of Surgeons in 1923. Words can, like drugs, change the way that a person thinks or feels, "entering into and coloring the minutest cells of the brain," he said. Can then the text typed in a message, for example, help you to quit smoking? Can their words improve your health through encouragement, education and well-timed reminders?

28

Stopping smoking

The "MiQuit" Study from the Universities of Cambridge, East Anglia and Nottingham showed that text messages sent during pregnancy could support some in smoking cessation, reducing risk to the unborn baby.

Over the course of 12 weeks women received texts including "motivational messages, advice about quit attempt preparation, managing cravings and withdrawal, dealing with trigger situations and preventing lapses, plus information about foetal development and how smoking affects this". On-demand support was available for combating cravings.

Self-management of diabetes

The "Sweet Talk Intervention" was a text message programme designed for people aged 8–18 wanting to better self-manage their diabetes. The young person would receive daily messages to reinforce and remind them of their goals in blood sugar control. They might, for example, be reminded to change their injection site if it felt lumpy, or to always test their sugar level if they felt unwell.

Users said that the messages helped them to learn new facts, test their sugars more — and gave them "encouragement to keep going".

Help for mother and baby

Delivering more than 250 text messages to pregnant women and mothers with infants under the age of one, the "Text4baby" app in the US provides medically accurate health education and lifestyle advice to help keep mum and baby healthy.

"Baby weighs about THREE pounds now. Over the next ten weeks, most babies gain another four or more pounds! More info on baby's growth ..."

"If you have any signs of preterm labour-cramps, belly tightening, low back pain, bleeding, or watery, pink/brown discharge, call the doctor right away," read some of the messages. Other advice includes how to wear a seatbelt, and emotional support. One mother said that the messages helped her to know that someone cares.

Reminders about meetings and medications

Each year, more than 15 million patients in the UK fail to turn up to general practice appointments, costing the NHS more than £216 million. In one study of more than 16,000 patients, text message reminders made people 23% more likely to attend clinic (though the "no show" rate was still 15%).

In "ARemind" (a "personalised system to remind for adherence"), text messages on a chosen subject (including latest news, weather, jokes, Bible verses and sport updates) were sent to people with HIV to remind them to take their antiretroviral therapy. Recipients were asked to respond with a text message when taking the tablets.

The texts achieved their target — at least in the short-term, and were more successful than a simple beeper instead being sounded at tablet time.

Lifestyle advice

A global collaboration known as "Text2PreventCVD" studied the results of 9 clinical trials, involving 3,779 participants, where text messages were sent for 6 months (in 7 studies) or for 12 months or 24 months.

Messages provided health information, motivation, lifestyle recommendations and support; modest impacts on blood pressure and body mass index were seen — and both are risk factors for heart disease. "Text messaging offers confidential and unobtrusive support," write the authors.

Privacy and potential

Some patients will not be comfortable with mobile messaging, concerned about breaches of confidentiality and privacy. Writing in the *British Medical Journal*, student in digital health Laura Martinengo explains the need for a login by way of password or biometric authentication (such as face or finger print recognition), and a mobile messaging service that complies with data protection laws.

The World Health Organization describes how, in many places, people are more likely to have access to a mobile telephone than to clean water. Their "Be he@lthy, Be mobile" initiative harnesses the power and reach of mobile phones to help people across the world make healthier lifestyle choices, with the aim of preventing and managing diseases such as cancer, diabetes and heart disease.

Total words: 837

Total Reading Time: _____ minutes _____ seconds

💬 **Vocabulary** -

hail *v.* 称颂……为……; 招手(请出租车或公共汽车停下); 跟……打招呼

stethoscope *n.* 听诊器

inroad *n.* (尤指通过消耗或削弱其他事物取得的)进展

minute *n.* 分钟; 一会儿, 瞬间; 时刻

    adj. 极小的, 微小的; 详细的, 细致入微的

well-timed *adj.* 适时的; 正合时宜的

cessation *n.* 停止; 终止; 中断

motivational *adj.* 有动机的; 激发性的

withdrawal *n.* 撤走; 收回; 退出

lapse *n.* 小错, 过失; 疏忽; 间隔时间

foetal *adj.* 胎儿的; 胎的

on-demand *adj.* 按需

diabetes *n.* 糖尿病

lumpy *adj.* 多块状物的

preterm *adj.* (婴儿)早产的

antiretroviral *adj.* 抗逆转录病毒

beeper *n.* 传呼机

confidential *adj.* 机密的，保密的

unobtrusive *adj.* 不张扬的；不招摇的

harness *v.* 控制，利用（以产生能量等）

Phrases

make inroads into 削弱，消耗

Notes

NHS: NHS refers to the National Health Service, which is the umbrella term for the publicly funded health care systems of the United Kingdom.

Rudyard Kipling: Rudyard Kipling(30 December 1865–18 January 1936) was an English journalist, short-story writer, poet, and novelist. He was born in India, which inspired much of his work.

biometric authentication: Biometric authentication is a user identity verification process that involves biological input, or the scanning or analysis of some part of the body.

Exercises

I. **Answer the following questions after reading the text.**

1. According to the text, what did the government use cellphones to do during the pandemic?

2. What does the author quote Rudyard Kipling's saying for?

3. Why will some patients not be content with mobile messaging?

4. What does the phrases "no show" mean in the text?

5. Why are people more likely to use a mobile telephone than clean water in many places according to WHO?

II. **Decide whether the following statements are true or false according to the text.**

1. From the text we can learn that Rudyard Kipling fully affirmed the function of mobile phones.

2. According the "MiQuit" Study, text messages help a married man to stop smoking, which keeps his wife and the baby healthy during pregnancy.

3. The "Text4baby" app can provide medical support as well as emotional support.

4. Text message reminders help the NHS reduce loss caused from patients' not attending

clinic.

5. According to the text, the author is not optimistic about the potential of mobile phones.

III. **Fill in the blank of the following sentences with one of the words or phrases given below. Change the form where necessary.**

harness	minute	hail	inroad	unobtrusive
motivation	confidential	lapse	withdraw	cessation

1. This problem could also lead to isolation from peers or _____ from activities, which could increase the risk for depression.
2. Employees in the firm are fully aware that they are not to use _____ information for the purposes of insider dealing.
3. So pure and yet teeming with cultural meanings, white is simultaneously _____ and attention getting.
4. They argued that the country should be _____ its natural resources and should be a net exporter of power rather than an importer.
5. Emotions are the organized psychobiological responses linking physiological, cognitive, and _____ systems.
6. The campaign was successful and now Coke is making _____ into what was once a market void.
7. In some places this process was for a time so _____ and insignificant that it escaped detection.
8. Usually war begins with the outbreak of hostilities and ends with their _____.
9. Opting against _____ a taxi, the lady took the car, figuring that she needed some practice.
10. Things can go wrong with the rope, and there can be a _____ of concentration.

IV. **Translate the following sentences into Chinese.**
1. Used to educate and motivate, to remind and to record, mobile telephones are making inroads into health care.

2. Can then the text typed in a message, for example, help you to quit smoking? Can their words improve your health through encouragement, education and well-timed

reminders?

3. In one study of more than 16,000 patients, text message reminders made people 23% more likely to attend clinic (though the "no show" rate was still 15%).

4. Some patients will not be comfortable with mobile messaging, concerned about breaches of confidentiality and privacy.

5. The World Health Organization describes how, in many places, people are more likely to have access to a mobile telephone than to clean water.

V. Select one word for each blank from the following word bank. You may not use any of the words in the bank more than once. Change the form where necessary.

exhaust	consume	opportunity	overwhelm	incorporate
harm	exercise	develop	nature	normal

Stress is a negative reaction that the body has to various factors and events. It is often caused by poor health and then leads to various health problems.

Having said that, stress is not all bad, it is a ___1___ bodily reaction to problems and complex tasks, for example, performing at work. This kind of stress is considered short-term. It passes quickly after solving difficulties without ___2___ the body. However, frequent emotional stresses may cause chronic stress, which, in turn, ___3___ into phobias and internal conflicts.

To minimize the chances of being ___4___ by stress and anxiety, it is worth considering different methods of dealing with this condition and how they are used in everyday life. Both a variety of psychological techniques and useful products are used to improve one's well-being.

Incorporate sports into your life

If you are often stressed and not ___5___ , this is the very sign to start exercising. Many people give up exercise at a young age because they think that only a heavyweight gym and a personal trainer are effective. But this is certainly not the case and there are plenty of ways to ___6___ exercise into your everyday life in an enjoyable manner:

- Swimming and exercise in water like Aqua Aerobics;
- Dancing (don't limit yourself to one style!);
- Running or walking (exercise truly can be a walk in the park);
- Active team games (can also be a great way to socialize which can greatly alleviate stress).

This is just a small list of what you can do to produce the happiness hormone and add a spring to your step. Contrary to the opinion that sport is ___7___ and doesn't leave any energy for other activities, for many this is a perfect way to overcome stress and gain strength for the whole day.

If you don't want to visit a gym for classes, simply get out into ___8___ with your friends and family, it really doesn't have to feel like a chore. In addition to improving your physical condition and health, you'll gain countless endorphins from the social muscles you don't even have to think about flexing.

Consume less alcohol and coffee

Not many people are able to completely give up a cup of coffee in the morning or a glass of wine after a long day at work, but everything should be taken in moderation. If you are often stressed and in these times ___9___ a lot of alcohol or coffee, the path to headaches and constant fatigue will be significantly shorter. Get rid of the habit of drinking coffee several times a day and drinking a bit too much with friends at every given ___10___ — the result will change your mental and physical state in countless ways.

Part III Extensive Reading

Text B

Do You Have Social Jet Lag? Here's What to Do

Do you love to stay up late and then catch up on sleep on the weekend or a day off? If so, you could be committing a social *faux pas* — when it comes to your sleep that is.

Called "social jet lag" by sleep scientists, it's the delay in your body's natural sleep clock that occurs when you stay up late on Friday and Saturday nights to socialize and then sleep in to catch up.

"Just like the way traveling from New York to Los Angeles can sometimes wreak havoc on your circadian rhythm (your body's natural clock), so too can staying up late at the end of a stressful work week and sleeping in on weekends," said sleep specialist Dr. Raj Dasgupta, an assistant professor of clinical medicine at the Keck School of Medicine at the University of Southern California.

"By staying up late on Friday and Saturday nights and sleeping in both days afterward, you're essentially forcing your body into a different time zone," Dasgupta said. "This pattern of sleeping puts you at risk for the effects of chronic sleep deprivation, which can put you at increased risk for medical conditions such as diabetes and heart disease."

You can further disrupt your sleep rhythm and add to your sleep debt by also staying up later during the workweek. Some of us can't help it. If you instinctively prefer to go to bed later and wake up later, you may be a "night owl".

It's possible that night owls are genetically predisposed to late nights due to a gene called CRY1, experts say. A recent study found a variance in CRY1 in people with delayed sleep phase disorder, or DSPD, a disorder in which people stay up extremely late and get up much later.

That might have been a problem in a preindustrial society with little light after dark, but today's world is full of light, sound and tons of nightlife — so what's the problem? Unfortunately, most work and school schedule are built for those who love to be "early to bed, early to rise".

"Keeping an owl schedule in our modern world with relatively early work (or school) schedule demands is less healthy," said sleep specialist Kenneth Wright, a professor of integrative psychology at the University of Colorado Boulder.

The danger of social jet lag

Changing your internal body clock or circadian rhythm by one to two hours confuses the body and brain. When it no longer knows what time to go to sleep and what time to get up, the body responds with such symptoms as insomnia, early waking or excessive sleepiness, daytime fatigue, difficulty concentrating, constipation or diarrhea, and an overall feeling of not being well.

A study published in May analyzed the sleep habits of 85,000 people in the UK and found those people with a misaligned sleep cycle were more likely to report depression, anxiety and have fewer feelings of well-being.

"Defying our internal body clock appears to be highly associated with levels of depression, and having a higher misalignment was associated with higher odds of depression," study author Dr. Jessica Tyrrell, a senior lecturer at the University of Exeter Medical School in the UK, told CNN in a prior interview.

On the other hand, people who love to get up early — often called "morning larks" — were less likely to have irregular sleep timing. And here's the kicker — the study found they were happier than night owls.

"If you're a morning person, then you are less likely to have depression and more likely to report a higher well-being. This may in part be due to the fact that people who are morning people are less likely to have 'social jet lag'," Tyrrell explained.

How to cure social jet lag

The cure? It's much like the patient who told the doctor: "It hurts when lifting my arm."

That's simple, the doctor replied:"Stop lifting your arm."

"Instead of waking and sleeping at times that are out of sync with your internal clock and shifting between two different sleep schedules (one for weekdays and one for weekends), try to maintain a healthy and consistent sleep schedule," Dasgupta said.

Go to sleep at the same general time each night, and wake at the same general time each morning, even on weekends. Of course, that's easier said than done for people who are born to be night owls. But it is possible, according to a 2019 randomized clinical trial that taught a group of night owls to rework their sleep habits.

Over a six-week period, 22 confirmed night owls were told to try to do the following:

● Go to sleep two to three hours before their habitual bedtime and wake up two to three hours before their typical wake up time.

● Keep their sleep and wake times the same (within 15 to 30 minutes) on work and free days.

● Get as much outdoor light exposure during the mornings as they could and limit light exposure at night.

● If they exercise, do it in the morning.

● Have breakfast as soon after wake up as possible, eat lunch and dinner at the same time every day — but don't eat dinner after 7 p.m.

● Don't drink caffeine after 3 p.m., and don't nap after 4 p.m.

At the end of the six weeks, researchers found that people who most closely followed the recommendations were able to push back their biological clocks by up to two hours, meaning they consistently went to bed and woke up two hours earlier. In addition, people reported less depression and stress. Tests of their cognitive reaction time and physical grip strength showed their performance in both areas peaked earlier in the day.

Other techniques

Of course, not everyone is a "night owl". Some of us are overwhelmed by work and school demands or simply practice poor sleep habits and suffer the consequences. A focus on good sleep hygiene will help train your brain to get your body clock back in sync.

Be sure to eliminate all bright lights, as even the blue light of cellphones or laptops can be disruptive. If that's hard to accomplish, think about using eye shades and blackout curtains to keep the room dark.

Try to eliminate disturbing sounds as well. Earplugs or white noise machines can be very helpful, but you can create your own with a humidifier or fan.

Other suggestions for good sleep include avoiding stimulants such as nicotine or coffee after midafternoon, especially if you have insomnia. Alcohol is another no-no. You may think it helps you doze off, but you are more likely to wake in the night as your body begins to process the spirits.

Also avoid rich, fatty foods just before sleep. If you have any digestive issues, eating fried or fatty foods, spicy meals, some citrus, and even carbonated drinks can trigger heartburn and indigestion.

Exercise is key to promoting good sleep. According to the National Sleep Foundation, as little as 10 minutes a day of walking, biking or other aerobic exercise can "drastically improve nighttime sleep quality".

Follow all these steps, and you'll be well on your way to fixing your social jet lag and improving your health.

Total words: 1,282

Total Reading Time: _____ minutes _____ seconds

Vocabulary

wreak *v.* 破坏；损坏

havoc *n.* 灾害，混乱

circadian *adj.* 昼夜节律的；生理节奏的

chronic *adj.* (疾病)慢性的，长期的；难以治愈(或根除)的

deprivation *n.* 贫困，缺乏，剥夺

instinctively *adv.* 本能地

predispose *v.* 使倾向于，使受……的影响

variance *n.* 变化幅度，差额

preindustrial *adj.* 工业化前的；未工业化的

insomnia *n.* 失眠(症)

fatigue *n.* 疲劳；厌倦

constipation *n.* 便秘

diarrhea *n.* 腹泻

misaligned *adj.* 方向偏离的；未对准的

defy *v.* 违抗，反抗；蔑视；无法相信、解释等；经受住

lark *n.* 云雀；百灵鸟

sync *n.* 同步；一致；协调

randomize *v.* 使随机化；(使)作任意排列

earplug *n.* (用以防噪声或防水的)耳塞

humidifier *n.* 加湿器

stimulant *n.* 兴奋剂；有激励作用的事物

nicotine *n.* 尼古丁

citrus *n.* 柑橘类水果

carbonated *adj.* 含二氧化碳的

heartburn *n.* (不消化引起的)烧心

indigestion *n.* 消化不良(症)

Phrases

faux pas [法]失礼,失态
wreak havoc(on) 给……造成破坏
in sync 同时
eye shade 遮光眼罩
blackout curtain 遮光帘
doze off(尤指在日间)打瞌睡,打盹儿

Exercises

I. Answer the following questions after reading the text.

1. What does "social jet lag" refer to?

2. According to Dasgupta, what are the consequences of successively staying up late in two days and sleeping in both days afterward?

3. What is the probable reason for some people who instinctively prefer to go to bed later and wake up later?

4. According to the study published in May in the UK, what problems of mental health will be more likely to rise as for people with a misaligned sleep cycle?

5. Why are morning people less likely to have depression, compared with night owls?

II. Decide whether the following statements are true or false according to the text.

1. The loss caused from staying up late can be retrieved through catching up on sleep for equivalent time.

2. A gene called CRY1 possibly makes the night owls get used to staying up late and will not bring forth health problems.

3. According to the study, the sleep disorder is often in direct proportion to depression.

4. All kinds of noises including white noise are harmful for people's health.

5. Alcohol may help you fall asleep in a shorter time but result in waking earlier.

III. Fill in the blanks with the words given in the brackets. Change the form where necessary.

1. Online lotteries, by their aggressive marketing techniques, has usually _____ (wreak) havoc on many families, especially those of daily-wage earners.

2. Blood pressure can notoriously come on and present itself when people have strokes or heart attacks as a result of a _____ (chronic) raised pressure.

3. They hope that it serves as a timely reminder for all of them of what a very great loss it is when people are _____ (deprivation) of their liberty.

4. Whether you're conscious of it or not, you have an _____ (instinctively) way of

approaching color.

5. All of them agreed that it is difficult to lead the masses anywhere — unless they are _____ (predispose) to head in that direction anyway.

6. Unless and until we make such a decision the law should be enforced against those individuals who openly _____ (defy) it whether here or abroad.

7. Both of them were in _____ (sync) about the idea and it made the whole process very easy.

8. The unexpected discovery of this cycle has _____ (stimulant) much interest in the field as well as in the popular press.

9. It has a very strong position in this country, with 60% of the _____ (carbonate) soft drinks market.

10. The father stayed with his little daughter until she fell asleep but at that point, he ended up _____ (doze) off as well.

IV. **Translate the following sentences into Chinese.**

1. Called "social jet lag" by sleep scientists, it's the delay in your body's natural sleep clock that occurs when you stay up late on Friday and Saturday nights to socialize and then sleep in to catch up.

2. This pattern of sleeping puts you at risk for the effects of chronic sleep deprivation, which can put you at increased risk for medical conditions such as diabetes and heart disease.

3. Unfortunately, most work and school schedule are built for those who love to be "early to bed, early to rise".

4. When it no longer knows what time to go to sleep and what time to get up, the body responds with such symptoms as insomnia, early waking or excessive sleepiness, daytime fatigue, difficulty concentrating, constipation or diarrhea, and an overall feeling of not being well.

5. Also avoid rich, fatty foods just before sleep. If you have any digestive issues, eating fried or fatty foods, spicy meals, some citrus, and even carbonated drinks can trigger heartburn and indigestion.

V. Topics for discussion.

1. Nowadays, many Chinese college students love to have lazy mornings for relaxing during summer or winter holidays. What do you think of that?

2. Many people argue that "you should not put off until tomorrow what you can do today", so they prefer to finish their tasks in a day on all accounts even if they staying up too late. What about your point of view on this way of doing things?

4 Life-style

Pre-reading Questions

1. Why do Chinese brides favour the phoenix-tail red gown?
2. Why do Western brides prefer white wedding dresses to red ones?
3. Do you know where makeup possibly originated?
4. On what occasions will you wear makeup?

Part II **Intensive Reading**

Text A

A History of Wedding Dresses

Steeped in cultural tradition, wedding dresses are so much more than lengthy trains and white lace frills. Jenessa Williams goes back to the beginning to find out more about the different ways in which Western culture perceives the garment.

Origins of the wedding dress

According to historians, the concept of donning a special garment for the purposes of marriage is thought to have originated in Chinese fable, where a princess was dressed in a phoenix dress and crown which would bring her luck and fortitude in the marriage. To this day, Chinese brides still favour a dramatic phoenix-tail red gown, a talisman homage to that early story.

In Korea and Japan, silk wedding robes changed in style according to the ruling dynasty and season, but normally adhered to bright colours, designed to emulate royalty.

Though the concept of marriage union stems back to the ancient civilizations of Sumer, Babylon and Assyria, the idea of weddings as a romantic notion is much more recent. Through analysis of paintings made from Assyrian artefacts (including British painter Edwin Long's 1875 interpretation), women would dress in draped garments of white or cream to be bid on in

41

a market-like environment, with the less desirable women being allocated to "commoners".

In Ancient Rome, brides wore braided hairstyles and veils of deep yellow, whereas Ancient Athenian women dressed in violets and reds, shaped by a girdle that would be symbolically loosened by the groom after a union.

Some believe that the wedding tradition of white stems from this marriage-market tradition, but it is just as likely that it was solidified within the Victorian age, steeped in connotations of virginity and purity. Costly and difficult to keep clean, white garments had appeared as a status symbol in various British weddings throughout the 1400s and 1500s, but when Queen Victoria wore a white gown to be married in 1840, the notion of a white wedding dress became the standard of the Western world.

Until Queen Victoria, the idea of purchasing a wedding dress to wear once simply wasn't an option. The queen herself re-used both her dress and veil, and many non-royal women would have simply used their Sunday best, or else dyed and altered a new gown for subsequent re-use. But with the industrial revolution and the rise of photography, the emphasis on a "one time only" dream gown became stronger, with white looking particularly striking in the new monochrome or sepia technology.

As a result, even the shape of Victoria's gown became the standard fashion for a bridal silhouette — a nipped-in waist, wide skirt and layers of ivory lace. Even the bridesmaids got in on the action; in fact, it was fairly typical for the bride and her bridal party to wear extremely similar gowns, potentially stemming from ancient Roman folklore that the similarity would confuse the curse of any lingering evil spirits.

As the 1900s wore on, the Edwardian era heralded a slightly more laid-back style, with looser gowns made from delicate fabrics. High necks, ruffles and long sleeves were a priority, as well as the emergence of elaborate headpieces and bouquets. Slowly but surely, we were beginning to see signs of women choosing shapes that they felt comfortable in, no longer adhering to a singular vision of the "perfect" bride.

Wedding dresses in the 1940s and 1950s

During the war effort, lavish gowns weren't exactly a priority for garment production. Instead, women returned to wearing their Sunday best, or occasionally, donning altered versions of their husband's suits, very much in keeping with the "make do and mend" mentality of the era.

Though the war was over by the time Queen Elizabeth married Prince Phillip in 1947, the country was still feeling the effects of rationing, and the mood was sombre. Wanting not to appear too overwhelming decadent, Elizabeth's dress of ivory silk and pearl was noticeably understated in comparison to her forebears, but would go on to be highly influential for the romantic bride, looking for delicate features like a shorter skirt or embroidered flowers to appear as youthful and feminine as possible.

Wedding dresses from the 1960s to 1980s

In keeping with the Free Love movement, white was no longer the only option in the

1960s. The famous canary yellow dress and flower crown that Elizabeth Taylor wore to marry Richard Burton comes to mind, but so do coat dresses and getaway outfits, designed in practical cotton fabrics and simple shapes to allow the bride to head straight off on her honeymoon.

Through all the subversions of the 1970s — peasant dresses, floppy hats instead of veils and bell sleeves — women were moving further and further away from the traditional hoop skirted silhouette of classic bridal fashion, but they were transported right back on the 29th July 1981, when Princess Diana stepped out of St. Paul's Cathedral in enormous taffeta. With 750 million people watching, she resembled every inch of the "more is more" aesthetic of the 1980s, putting oversized bows, lace and puff sleeves firmly back on the wedding map.

Wedding dresses in the 1990s and 2000s

With so much history to draw on, the westernized wedding dress had been back and forth so many times that the form had almost been perfected, with brides knowing inherently whether they were a "big-skirted" or a more laid-back type of woman.

In 1990, Vera Wang opened her first bridal boutique, popularizing the strapless, form-fitting gown that was normally accessorized with a slicked-back up-do and silver accessories. Though wedding dresses had appeared at fashion couture shows since the late 1950s, it was becoming more and more regular in the 1990s fashion weeks and showrooms, with designers such as Calvin Klein, Versace and Oscar De La Renta all offering their own signature take on a formal occasion dress.

The popularity of reality TV also played its part in the bridal wear boom. Shows like *Say Yes to the Dress*, *Don't Tell the Bride* and *Big Fat Gypsy Weddings* all increased our interest in what it takes to put on a very special day, often with the gown as a be-all-and-end-all focus. Hints of this would continue into the 2010s, but the rise of social media would also offer it's alternatives ...

Wedding dresses from the 2010s to now

Though the UK wedding industry is worth more than ever (approximately £14.7 billion), we are all learning that there is no right way to wear a wedding dress. With changing laws around civil partnerships as well as an increased understanding of modern feminism and gender expression, the desire to do bridal wear has ranged from caped-jumpsuits to matching suits and indeed anything that makes the wearer feel special.

In keeping with this push for inclusivity, the late 2000s and early 2010s also saw an increase in bridal blogging and online communities, helping "alternative" brides to find the perfect outfit for them. Sites such as Rock N Roll Bride, Love My Dress and Nu Bride have shown that tradition looks very different to different cultures, and the high-street seems to be following suit, offering affordable wedding attire that is accessible to various body types and budgets.

Even ASOS has gotten in on the action, selling a range of Indian-inspired bridal wear that seeks to recognize wedding attire outside of the typical Anglo-Christian lens. Though there is some critique in the inexpensive appropriation of a garment so rooted in extensive symbolism and hand-made embellishment, the recognition that weddings don't always fit a singular culture tradition is an important one for British retail. The coronavirus pandemic will have likely also played a part, with many couples stripping back the detail of their outfits to focus on a small-scale event.

As with any fashion garment, certain styles still very much pervade. Just this month, American pop singer Ariana Grande got married in a Vera Wang gown and bow-topped veil that would have been entirely befitting of the glamorous 1960s bride, while Princess Beatrice's private 2020 wedding saw the bride wearing vintage, handed down to her by the Queen and modernized with the addition of 1970s chiffon sleeves. Wherever we are in history, it seems bridal wear will always appreciate its "something borrowed" — a taste as bespoke as the romantic union it symbolizes.

Total words: 1,413

Total Reading Time: _____ minutes _____ seconds

💬 Vocabulary

steep *v.* 深深浸淫；饱含（某品质）
　　adj. (斜坡、山等)陡峭的
frill *n.* 饰边；褶边
lace *n.* 网眼织物；蕾丝；花边
garment *n.* 衣服
don *v.* 穿上
fable *n.* 寓言；寓言故事；谎言
phoenix *n.* 凤凰
fortitude *n.* 勇气，胆量，刚毅
talisman *n.* 护身符；驱邪物
homage *n.* 敬辞；表示敬意的举动
emulate *v.* 仿真，模仿；努力赶上；同……竞争
artefact *n.* 人工制品，手工艺品
drape *v.* 悬挂，披；遮盖
commoner *n.* 平民
girdle *n.* 腰带；围绕物
solidify *v.* (使)凝固，变硬；变得结实
monochrome *adj.* 单色的；黑白的
sepia *n.* 乌贼墨颜料（或墨汁）；深褐色制品
　　adj. 乌贼墨色的
silhouette *n.* 剪影；暗色轮廓
linger *v.* 继续存留，缓慢消失；流连，逗留

herald *v.* 预示；宣布

lavish *adj.* 大量的；给人印象深刻的，耗资巨大的

embroider *v.* 刺绣；加以渲染（或润色）

subversion *n.* 颠覆；破坏

taffeta *n.* 塔夫绸

resemble *v.* 像，看起来像

laid-back *adj.* 安详放松的；松弛的；仿佛无忧无虑的

westernize *v.* 使西方化

popularize *v.* 推广，使普及；宣传

strapless *adj.* 无吊带的；无肩带的

attire *n.* 服装；衣服

pervade *v.* 遍及；弥漫

befitting *adj.* 适合的

glamorous *adj.* 独特的；特别富有魅力的

Phrases

in keeping with 与……一致

bridal wear 婚纱

back and forth 来回地，反复地

Notes

Queen Victoria: Queen Victoria was the queen of Great Britain and Ireland from 1837 to 1901. She used the additional title of Empress of India from 1 May 1876.

Edwardian: era: The Edwardian era refers to Edwardian period of British history that spanned the reign of King Edward VII, from 1901 to 1910. It was the last period of British history to be named after the reigning monarch.

Vera Wang: Vera Wang (王薇薇；born June 27, 1949) is an American fashion designer and of Chinese descent. She is well-known for her wide range of haute couture bridesmaid gowns and wedding gown collections, as well as for her clientele of elite ladies figure skaters, designing dresses for competitions and exhibitions.

Exercises

I. **Answer the following questions after reading the text.**

1. According to historians, where did the concept of wearing the wedding dress

probably originate from?

2. Why did people prefer bright colour of silk wedding robes in Korea and Japan?

3. What events prompted the notion of a white wedding dress to become the standard of the Western world?

4. What is the distinctive feature of history backgrounds with regards to wedding dresses in the 1940s and 1950s?

5. What is the changing trend of wedding dresses from the 2010s to now?

II. **Decide whether the following statements are true or false according to the text.**

1. According to the text, Chinese brides still love a dramatic phoenix-tail red gown, just because of its exquisite craftsmanship.

2. People had already purchased wedding dresses prior to Queen Victoria.

3. Women started to take a pragmatic approach to choosing wedding dresses in the Edwardian era.

4. Women started to choose wedding dresses of other colors apart from white ones from the 1960s to 1980s.

5. From the history of wedding dresses, we can infer that wedding dresses have been evolving into diversification.

III. **Fill in the blank of the following sentences with one of the words or phrases given below. Change the form where necessary.**

emulate	fortitude	inclusivity	glamorous	resemble
don	lavish	popularize	steep	linger

1. Apart from walking you to school, he even _____ around for you to change and walk you home.

2. The program did much to _____ little-known singers.

3. Where homes once stood, there were scenes _____ an earthquake zone.

4. During the Song Dynasty in ancient China, _____ decorated books were produced using woodblocks.

5. Last month's mystery wedding picture showed a _____ dressed couple in their middle years, who could well have been foreign.

6. Once each day, you leave the park, every time with a greater reluctance for _____ your shirt.

7. Knowing she is _____ her mother's behavior, Tom cannot stop thinking — she is driven by fear.

8. The old man died peacefully after a short illness borne with characteristic courage and _____.

9. It's about raising bigger questions of diversity and _____ that haven't been raised.

10. The surrounding area is _____ in culture and history with many historical sites worthy of a visit nearby.

IV. Translate the following sentences into Chinese.

1. Though the concept of marriage union stems back to the ancient civilizations of Sumer, Babylon and Assyria, the idea of weddings as a romantic notion is much more recent.

2. Costly and difficult to keep clean, white garments had appeared as a status symbol in various British weddings throughout the 1400s and 1500s, but when Queen Victoria wore a white gown to be married in 1840, the notion of a white wedding dress became the standard of the Western world.

3. As a result, even the shape of Victoria's gown became the standard fashion for a bridal silhouette — a nipped-in waist, wide skirt and layers of ivory lace.

4. Though the UK wedding industry is worth more than ever (approximately £14.7 billion), we are all learning that there is no right way to wear a wedding dress.

5. Wherever we are in history, it seems bridal wear will always appreciate its "something borrowed" — a taste as bespoke as the romantic union it symbolizes.

V. Select one word for each blank from the following word bank. You may not use any of the words in the bank more than once. Change the form where necessary.

relaxing	boost	dual	paint	embarrass
stigma	fight	professional	mental	depression

With hairdressers and barbers reopening, millions of people across the UK have been able to breathe a sigh of relief. For some, it's a welcome end to disastrous home trims and colouring catastrophes.

But for others, a visit to the barber or salon means much more than an Angled Bob or a Textured Crop. For people struggling with __1__ health problems, the salon chair can be a safe space to talk about their lives and open up about their problems.

Prior to the pandemic, the UK was already dealing with large numbers of issues related to mental health. Figures released in 2016 showed that 1 in 6 adults experienced a mental health problem like anxiety or __2__ every week. The same study showed that 1 in 5 adults had considered suicide at some point in their lives. While the final effect of the pandemic on the nation's mental health will not be known for some time (COVID-19 will generate countless scientific and sociological research papers and many forests-worth of books), emerging studies are __3__ a bleak picture. Towards the end of 2020, modelling suggested that as many as 10 million people in England alone will require new or additional mental health support due to the pandemic, many on a long-term basis.

Although millions will get the help they need, sadly huge numbers will not seek help at all. Despite the efforts of health care bodies, charities and other organizations, far too many of us think there's a __4__ associated with having a mental health problem. While wc'll probably have more need to talk about our mental health than ever before over the next few years to come, a lot of people will be too __5__ to go talk to their doctor. Although it might seem surprising, hairdressers and barbers are likely to be in the front line of support for people __6__ mental health issues.

It's well known that people go to the hairdresser when they want to __7__ their confidence with a new look for a new job, or to help to wash a failed relationship out of their hair. The feel-good benefits of a regular groom or pampering are also self-evident, but it is likely that there is much more to it than that too. The __8__ environment of a salon or barber shop can make it much easier for people to unburden themselves of their worries, while hairdressers tend to build strong relationships up with their clients, often over the course of many years.

As trust builds, barriers are broken down and people become willing to talk, and while they might feel a stigma of talking to a mental health __9__, it can be much easier to open up while sitting in a salon chair. Certainly, from financial worries and redundancies, to failing relationships and COVID problems, hairdressers and barbers hear it all. Often, the conversations can end up covering some challenging issues and tough subjects. A recent national survey by Booksy, the brilliant online appointment and schedule management app that makes booking and managing appointments easy for health and beauty businesses and their clients, found that 43% of hair professionals felt they were performing a __10__ role — a hairdresser and a therapist.

Part III   **Extensive Reading**

Text B

The Evolution of Makeup

As long as there have been people, there has been makeup and today, cosmetics can be found in almost every society on earth. Here's the history of humans and face paint.

The Ancient World

Egypt

Many cosmetic materials still popular today — including kohl and henna — were first used in ancient Egypt.

Men and women of all classes would decorate their eyes with coloured kohl, usually in dark green, black or blue. These kohl circles were supposed to ward off the evil eye.

Scientists now believe the lead in this makeup may even have kept wearers healthier, as it killed off bacteria.

We also know that Egyptians used castor oil as a protective balm and the Romans described them using creams consisting of beeswax, olive oil, rosewater and more.

The world's first anti-wrinkle serums were also used in ancient Egypt.

China

In ancient China, painting fingernails began circa 3,000 BCE as a way to establish social class.

Royals wore gold or silver while the lower classes were forbidden to wear bright nail colours.

Plum blossom makeup, which originated from a folklore about a princess whose beauty was enhanced when a petal fell on her face, was also popular throughout the Tang and Song dynasties (618–1279)

Japan

Geishas are still famous for their striking makeup. They originally used lipstick made from crushed safflower petals to paint their eyebrows and lips and rice powder to colour the face.

For official ceremonies, a black paint called ohaguro was (and still is) used to colour the teeth.

Europe

Even further back, Alexander the Great wore makeup for both aesthetic and health reasons. Eye makeup "protected the delicate skin around the eyes, kept off flies ... and sheltered the eyes from the sun's glare".

As he travelled around Asia, Alexander would send plant cuttings home to a friend in Athens so that they could create a garden especially for beauty products.

Ancient Britons were known by Romans as "picts" — the painted ones — because of the blue woad they daubed over their faces.

The 20th Century

During the 1900s, the lower classes were labourers who spent the majority of their time outdoors working the fields or selling their wares. As a result, they usually had tanned skin.

A pale complexion came to symbolize a gentrified or aristocratic person who did not have to work for their income. Makeup of the 1900s consequently sought to emulate this pale appearance.

Making your face white was a dangerous practice in the 1900s, as the main ingredient in powders was generally arsenic.

The cosmetic routine at this time involved a simple powdered face, pinching to bring colour to the cheeks, and darkening eyelashes with burnt matches. Coloured petals or wet red tissue paper were used to colour the lips.

With the movie industry boom, Hollywood began having a huge impact on popular cosmetics in the 1920s. Makeup artists of popular actresses dramatically influenced how the public used makeup, and it was at this time that big names such as Max Factor rose to prominence.

Designers followed Hollywood's lead, and Coco Chanel popularized a now classic look: dark eyes, red lipstick and a suntan.

The new, accessible approach to makeup hit a stumbling block during the Second World War as cosmetics were in short supply.

This didn't stop British women staying glamorous, however — after all, the government constantly reminded them that "beauty is a duty".

Beetroot was a popular supplement for lip stain and proved relatively harmless compared to the use of boot polish as mascara.

Perhaps the worst trend was the foundation concocted from a blend of margarine and chalk.

The rise of mainstream feminism in the 1960s and 1970s saw many women partaking in an anti-cosmetics movement. They claimed that makeup was a tool in objectification, which saw society treat women as sex objects rather than people.

Susan Brownmiller went so far as to call the unmade up face "the honourable new look of feminism".

Not all women felt this way however. In the 1970s Avon introduced the world to the lady saleswoman. Despite certain feminist misgivings, the general consensus was that the popularity of makeup provided opportunities for women as entrepreneurs, inventors, manufacturers and distributors.

The 1970s was a time of real boom for men wearing makeup. Inverting stereotypical gender roles was a symbol of counter-culture defiance. The Cure's frontman, Robert Smith, remembers, "I started growing my hair long and wearing makeup and stuff because I was at school and I wasn't allowed to."

The iconic makeup of rock band KISS became a staple of their stage presence in the 1970s as part of the New York "glitter movement".

Speaking about the inspiration behind their look to fanzine *Porkchops* and *Applesauce*, vocalist Gene Simmons said, "we knew we wanted to get outlandish — being on stage dressed like a bum wasn't my idea of respect."

Many other glam rock male performers including David Bowie, Alice Cooper and Iggy Pop began to wear more flamboyant makeup looks both on and off the stage.

With access to all makeup imaginable, 1980s looks featured bright eye shadows teamed with bold lipsticks and big hair — a style mastered by singers like Boy George and Madonna.

The 1990s brought normcore and grunge to the mainstream. Faces were either clean and natural or making a statement with heavily kohled eyes and dark lips.

Gwen Stefani, Courtney Love and Winona Ryder all worked the grunge look alongside Billie-Joe Armstrong, Kurt Cobain and Johnny Depp.

Today

In the 21st century, makeup is for everyone. Men are quickly catching onto products such as concealer and eyeliner to enhance their own features.

As gender equality movements progress, the line between who "can and can't" wear makeup is becoming ever more blurred. (or should that be blended?)

Now more than ever, makeup is seen as a tool of self-expression, whoever that self may be.

Total words: 1,049

Total Reading Time: _____ minutes _____ seconds

💬 Vocabulary

kohl *n.* 黑色眼影粉

henna *n.* 散沫花染剂

ward *v.* 防止、避免

　　 n. 病房,病室

bacteria *n.* (bacterium 的复数) 细菌

balm *n.* 香脂油

anti-wrinkle *adj.* 抗皱纹的

serum *n.* 血清;免疫血清

circa *prep.* 大约

petal *n.* 花瓣

crush *v.* 压碎,捣碎

safflower *n.* 红花

aesthetic *adj.* 审美的，美学的

daub *v.* 涂抹

gentrified *v.* 使……贵族化

aristocratic *adj.* 贵族的，有贵族特征的

arsenic *n.* 砒霜；砷

pinch *v.* 捏，拧，掐；捏住，夹紧

prominence *n.* 重要，著名；突出；卓越

mascara *n.* 睫毛膏

margarine *n.* 人造黄油

partake *v.* 吃，喝；享用；参与

concoct *v.* 配制，调合；调制

objectification *n.* 人格物化（把人当成没有权利和感情的物体）

misgiving *n.* 疑虑，顾虑

invert *v.* 使倒置，倒转；颠倒

defiance *n.* 违抗，反抗

fanzine *n.* （音乐、体育等方面的）爱好者杂志

outlandish *adj.* 古怪的；奇特的；极不寻常的

bum *n.* 流浪乞丐；无业游民

flamboyant *adj.* 艳丽的；炫耀的

grunge *n.* 脏东西；垃圾摇滚乐；垃圾摇滚风格

concealer *n.* 遮瑕膏，遮瑕霜

blur *v.* 使变模糊

Phrases

ward off 避开；挡开

stumble block 绊脚石

Notes

ohaguro: Ohaguro is known as teeth blackening in Japan. It existed in one form or another for hundreds of years, and was seen amongst the population as beautiful until the end of the Meiji period. Objects that were pitch black, such as glaze-like lacquer, were seen as beautiful at that time.

geisha: Geisha (in Kyoto and Kanazawa) are a class of female Japanese performance artists and entertainers trained in traditional Japanese performing arts styles, such as dance, music and singing, as well as being proficient conversationalists and hosts.

Max Factor: Max Factor is a line of cosmetics from Coty, Inc. It was founded in 1909 as Max Factor & Company by Maksymilian Faktorowicz, a beautician from Poland.

Exercises

I.   Answer the following questions after reading the text.

1. In which country or region in ancient world was makeup loaded with distinctive features of social hierarchy?
2. What were kohl circles probably used for by ancient Egyptian?
3. Why did people still make their face white even though this kind of makeup was a dangerous practice in the 1900s?
4. What does the phrase "hit a stumbling block" mean in the text?
5. What is today's trendy notion of makeup?

II.   Decide whether the following statements are true or false according to the text.

1. In ancient Egypt, people already learned to employ makeup to deal with anti-aging issues.
2. From the text we can infer that poor peasants in ancient China were allowed to wear bright nail colours.
3. Nowadays, Japanese still use ohaguro on the occasions of official ceremonies.
4. Early in the 1900s, people used cosmetics to make their skin look tanned because it was considered to be healthy.
5. During the Second World War, the government of UK encouraged women to do makeup.

III.   Fill in the blanks with the words given in the brackets. Change the form where necessary.

1. The girl put up a hand as if to _____ (ward) the man off.
2. Chopping devices are favoured over mincers because the latter tend to _____ (crushed) the meat, squeezing out the juices.
3. Women also appreciate the _____ (aesthetic) value of a knife and may choose to combine function with beauty.
4. Many of the family have lived in China for several years and some of them are very _____ (prominence) in business circles in the Shanghai area.
5. Yesterday they _____ (partake) in a meaningful activity and then dispersed at a given time.
6. They fool the simple folk by _____ (concoct) exciting stories about their receiving messages from the film.
7. We have no education, no money, no political empowerment and we have _____

(objectification) women to a level that is very degrading.

8. They are either in a minority or they are silent about their _____ (misgiving).

9. The lady carefully picked up two small bottles, _____ (concealer) one with the other.

10. The roof is essentially _____ (invert) or turned upside down compared to the standard roofing.

IV. Translate the following sentences into Chinese.

1. In ancient China, painting fingernails began circa 3,000 BCE as a way to establish social class.

2. Plum blossom makeup, which originated from a folklore about a princess whose beauty was enhanced when a petal fell on her face, was also popular throughout the Tang and Song dynasties (618–1279).

3. Eye makeup "protected the delicate skin around the eyes, kept off flies ... and sheltered the eyes from the sun's glare".

4. During the 1900s, the lower classes were labourers who spent the majority of their time outdoors working the fields or selling their wares. As a result, they usually had tanned skin.

5. As gender equality movements progress, the line between who "can and can't" wear makeup is becoming ever more blurred. (or should that be blended?)

V. Topics for discussion.

1. Someone argues that wearing makeup is to show respect to others. Do you agree? Why or why not?

2. Nowadays more and more men wear makeup. What do you think of the phenomenon?

Pre-reading Questions

1. Do you think food is an important part of people's life?
2. What do you think is the significance of traditional festivals about food?
3. What kinds of materials are qualified to be the ingredients of delicious food?
4. What do you think are the necessary elements to make a delicious meal?

Part II

Intensive Reading

Text A

Going Deep into Oyster Country

On the marsh-bound causeway to Chincoteague Island on Virginia's Eastern Shore, cars and their drivers seemed to float across the still waters of Queens Sound. As I made my way across, I thought of how, in centuries past, skiffs drifted through the region's bays, channels and coves in search of shellfish. Back then, before fish-farming became popular, the land itself functioned as a sort of natural pier for its residents who wrangled clams and oysters and terrapin, as thick as treasure, from beds in the brackish water.

My visit to Chincoteague last September was part of an exploration of an American tradition rich in history and lore. A few weeks after that trip, I would head to the opposite side of the Chesapeake, to Leonardtown, Md. — home of the St. Mary's County Oyster Festival and National Shucking Competition. On my journey through the region, I wanted to delve into something that had been a part of my childhood: the culture surrounding oysters. I was curious about the difference between the tradition, here, along the eastern Virginia coast, and in places like New York City and New Orleans, where I'm from. As an African-American and native Southerner, I also wanted to explore how Black culture figured in — to see if the world of oysters reflected something larger about the American experience across racial lines.

Years ago, growing up on Louisiana's Gulf Coast, I'd watch oyster shuckers, usually black men, popping open shell after shell, joking with guests on the opposite side of the bar while they worked. They reminded me of my uncles at our family seafood boil, who shared stories as they stood around an 80-quart pot. In New York and other cities to the north, the lifestyle surrounding oysters seemed altogether different, from the well-attired shuckers at fancy restaurants, down to the serving plates and wine pairings. I wanted to know more about this difference in attitude toward the shellfish and the kinds of experiences they conjured.

A black oysterman from coastal Virginia

Chincoteague was quiet on this clear blue day in September, but between the succession of seafood shacks and ice-cream parlors I felt the pulse of a town aware of its history. The regional boom in oysters that began in the mid-19th-century still hangs over the place whose nearness to waters that were once rich with oyster reefs allowed the industry to thrive.

I stopped at the town's museum, where I found rustic oyster tools and shells, and exhibits in the front room on the boats that were used for various maritime activities, such as duck hunting and shellfish dredging. Past the "Misty" exhibition (about a beloved wild pony), I fiddled with a pair of traditional oyster tongs, which are rarely used these days and resemble a pair of rakes slanted across one another and bolted together, and tried my hand at raking loose shells from beneath a mound of boxed-in sand.

In one corner, there was an area dedicated to the African-American experience on Chincoteague Island. I read through the text on the wall and then examined a photo of black men shucking oysters in an adjacent section. Strangely, I didn't come across any mention of one of the area's most famous black oystermen — Thomas Downing, who would eventually become the acclaimed proprietor of Downing's Oyster House, a 19th-century oyster cellar in New York City. Downing was born on Virginia's Eastern Shore in 1791 to a black family whose freedom had been granted after a travelling preacher convinced the Downing's slaveholder that it was bad faith to be both a member of the Methodist Church and hold enslaved people. Post-enslavement, the Downings stayed in Accomack County on the Virginia Shore and eventually acquired a small plot of land. The family became a part of the Chincoteague community where they were said to have regularly hosted prominent whites of the county before and after church on Sundays — a relationship that at least appeared to approach being neighborly, though it still evoked a resemblance to antebellum culture, in which enslaved black people cooked meals for white plantation families.

Historically, African-American neighborhoods were tucked away from the waterfront, so if you want to look for traces of the Downings' life on Chincoteague, you might go farther inland to higher ground where the Union Baptist and Christ United Methodist churches are. A local podcast series called "The Bivalve Trail" further describes Thomas

Downing's story on Chincoteague, following his journey all the way to New York.

Years after Downing learned to tong oysters on Virginia's Eastern Shore, the wider Chesapeake region became one of the largest producers of oysters in North America. That changed in the 1970s and 1980s when the annual harvest sharply declined from the more than 25 million pounds that Virginia and Maryland had been producing just a decade or so before. A combination of overharvesting as well as a surge of waterborne disease led to the depletion of the region's oyster reefs, which, despite ongoing efforts to revitalize them, are still far from their peak. Both Maryland and Virginia, once titans of wild oyster production, now turn out less than 250,000 pounds a year.

So it's not surprising that the region has pivoted to aquaculture. Oyster farmers have largely replaced oyster tongers, and while raising oysters doesn't replace the wonder that comes with unearthing shells from a wild reef, the practice allows farmers to protect oyster seed from predators, disease and even the simple threat of soft mud, which, given the absence of a hardened reef, could bury and suffocate an oyster.

In New York, a storied 19th-century oyster cellar

When Downing moved to New York City in 1819, he quickly became acquainted with the Hudson River, where he fixated on finding the best of the best on the New Jersey side of the river. Downing knew that oysters were sought after in New York, and he made friends fast and patrons faster. Eventually he opened his own cellar, Downing's Oyster House, on Broad Street in 1825, where he'd serve Charles Dickens and a whole world of white elites. Even Queen Victoria ate oysters sent to her by Downing.

The culture surrounding oysters started changing during the 19th century. There were the blue-collar oystermen that Downing left behind on Virginia's Eastern Shore, but New York City had its own oystermen who would transform their homes into dining cellars for those wanting a no-frills meal fresh from the sea.

When Downing arrived in New York, oyster cellars — many of them black-operated and supplied by black oystermen — were already popular, but they were not considered respectable places for serious dining. Downing believed that he could distinguish himself by appealing to the businessmen in the Financial District. With savings from years of working as an oysterman in Philadelphia and New York, he decorated his restaurant with damask curtains, a chandelier and fine carpeting. In the evening, businessmen would even bring their wives to Downing's, which was significant since oyster houses typically weren't thought of as "proper".

His restaurant flourished. The new dining haven signaled a shift in the way people perceived oysters, both as a food and social experience. It's this complexity in the cultural interpretation of oysters and the way they've been represented over time that fascinates me.

Smoked oysters, raw oysters and everything in between

About a month after my visit to Chincoteague, on a windy October afternoon, I walked through the gates of the St. Mary's County fairgrounds in Leonardtown, Md., to attend the county's annual oyster festival and national shucking competition. There seemed to be more beers and ball caps than you'd see at a baseball game. Lines snaked in various directions from the vendor tents whose offerings ranged from kettle corn and ice cream to smoked oysters, raw oysters and skewered bacon.

I tried the day's first pair of raw oysters in a tasting tent that featured craft beers alongside a bounty of regionally farmed oysters. The shuckers themselves worked as unpretentious ushers to the whole experience, prying open the oysters and revealing the glistening shellfish. The feeling was homey, relaxed, a far cry from the patina of luxury apparent in many places in the Northeast, a connoisseurs' arena, much like winemaking. Bluepoints (an oyster native to Long Island's Great South Bay) are as much of a brand name as Bordeaux, each denoting a region as a way to signify value and authenticity.

At the festival in St. Mary's County, there was little trace of those refined associations. On my second round, I picked up a half dozen oysters inside a barn where shuckers worked in a fluid line, and took my plate to the dining section, which consisted of standing tables constructed of thin plywood held up by sawhorses. Here, people leaned over their plates, dousing their oysters with hot sauce.

Back outside, I came across a man wearing a tall pair of waterproof, wide-mouthed shrimp boots. He looked like he'd just finished hauling oysters. With his shirt tucked into his jeans and his jeans tucked into his boots, he upturned a Bud Light can and sighed; I felt my own posture loosen as he quenched his thirst. To the right of him was a tailgate filled with empty shells.

The competition

Long before I'd ever tasted an oyster, I'd seen black men shuck them behind bars in New Orleans, talking up a storm as they flitted their knives as quickly as their wrists could manage. They always seemed to be the dressed-down stars of the evening. The tourists would laugh throughout the night, enjoying the service as much as what was on their plate. It was a part of the experience: to be in New Orleans was to be charmed by its locals, especially those who fit into neat caricatures — the street musician, the confectioner, the oyster shucker.

The oysters themselves are somewhat blander than the Northeastern fare with their crisp brininess. Since the Gulf of Mexico stays warm throughout the year, Gulf Coast oysters are softer. And since the Mississippi River flushes its freshwater at the foot of the Gulf's estuaries, the salinity of oysters is tame.

Chesapeake oysters are also considered mild on the spectrum of salinity, affected by the freshwater runoff from the James, Rapphannock, Potomac and Susquehanna rivers, which knocks the bay's oysters down the choice list of many connoisseurs.

But such analysis wasn't part of the scene at the St. Mary's County Oyster festival. As I settled into the wooden bleachers for the shucking competition, it was clear that for many this was the main event. The bleachers filled up quickly and others straddled the short fence that separated the crowd from the stage, which was decorated with the flags representing each of the states that the competitors had come from. Participants and crowd members who brought their own chairs and blankets convened on the other side of the fence in a field, and a local bluegrass band played off to the right.

The competition spanned two days. The first day had been cut short by bad weather; on the second, I traded bits of conversation with a woman sitting beside me. She and her husband, she said, were from the county and attended the festival every year, which she said had stayed pretty much the same. Many of the people on the stage were familiar to her, including a woman named Deborah Pratt, who was introduced as a champ who'd won the national competition at least four times.

Ms. Pratt, older now and equipped with an oxygen tank, received a warm welcome from the crowd as she took her place among the other competitors in the women's final. It was clear that she had become a fixture at the festival, which was celebrating its 55th year. As a black woman from Jamaica, Va., farther south along the Chesapeake, in a mostly white crowd, she appeared to be something of a star. Before the final commenced, she gave a speech where she seemed to announce her retirement, calling out farewells to the crowd before thanking the people who had, in her words, thrown their arms around her in protection as the lone black woman in competitions throughout the years. "Ain't everybody bad," she said. "There's a lot of good people in this crowd."

The moment was moving, but it did make me reflect on how much she'd likely endured or narrowly avoided in this part of Americana, something I could relate to as a black man there from out of town. I stayed wary, but was comfortable that in this setting, most negative sentiments would be contained.

Part of the tradition of the competition was that after a round of shucking was completed, the competitors would bring their tray of half shells to the fence where spectators would grab them for eating. The husband of the woman I had been sharing conversation with mentioned that watching the crowd fumble up to the fence with extended hands was an added layer of entertainment. And, for them, it was the only time they really ate oysters, the woman told me. Otherwise, oysters were just a part of the novelty of their town and too expensive to enjoy regularly.

Total words: 2,306

Total Reading Time: _____ minutes _____ seconds

💬 **Vocabulary** -

causeway *n.*（穿越水面或湿地的）堤道

skiff *n.* 小划艇；小帆船

drift *v.* 漂流，漂移；飘

cove *n.* 小海湾

pier *n.* 突堤码头

wrangle *v.* 争论；争吵

terrapin *n.* (北美的)淡水龟

lore *n.* 学问；传统；某一方面的学问

shuck *v.* 剥壳；去……的外皮

well-attired *adj.* 衣着考究的

conjure *v.* 使……呈现于脑际；使想起

shack *n.* 简陋的小屋；棚屋

rustic *adj.* 乡村的；淳朴的

dredging *n.* 疏浚；清淤

tongs *n.* 夹剪，煤钳

rake *n.* 耙子

slant *v.* (使)倾斜；歪斜

adjacent *adj.* 邻近的

proprietor *n.* 所有人，业主

cellar *n.* 地窖；地下室

antebellum *adj.* 战前岁月的；(尤指)美国内战前的

depletion *n.* 消耗；用尽

reef *n.* 暗礁

unearth *v.* 发掘；挖掘

suffocate *v.* (使)窒息而死，(把……)闷死

no-frills *adj.* 不提供多余服务的；不加装饰的

damask *n.* 锦缎；花缎

fairground *n.* 露天游乐场；农畜产品集市场地

skewer *v.* 用扦子串住

vendor *n.* 小贩；卖主；销售公司

patina *n.* (木器或皮革的)光泽

connoisseur *n.* 鉴赏家，鉴定家；行家

denote *v.* 表示，标志；预示

sawhorse *n.* 锯木架

douse *v.* 浇灭(火)；熄(灯)

brininess *n.* 咸度

estuary *n.* (江河入海的)河口；河口湾

salinity *n.* 盐分，盐度

tame *adj.* 平淡无奇的；枯燥乏味的；驯服的

straddle *v.* 跨坐；分腿站立；跨过；横跨

wary *adj.* 小心的；谨慎的；小心翼翼的

Phrases

brackish water 微咸水；半咸水；淡盐水（盐分界于河海水之间）

delve into 钻研

hang over 挂在……之上

fiddle with 乱动，摆弄；玩弄

tuck away 把……隐匿

pivot to 以……为重点；转向……

fixate on 固定；专注于……

Notes

St. Mary's County Oyster Festival and National Shucking Competition: Since 1967, the County has been celebrating the U.S. Oyster Festival and the opening of the oyster season on the Chesapeake Bay with the US National Oyster Shucking Championship and National Oyster Cook-off. Known for its exquisite range of seafood and exhibition of cultural activities surrounding oysters and the waterman's way of life in St. Mary's County, this annual festival also includes live music, local foods, arts, crafts, craft beer tasting, and general family fun. The National Shucking Championship includes competitors from all over the United States competing for the title of US Oyster Shucking Champion. The US winner then goes on to compete in Galway, Ireland for the World Shucking Championship.

Methodist Church: The United Methodist Church is a collection of associated congregations of Protestantism whose doctrine and beliefs are motivated by the spirit and teachings of John Wesley. George Whitefield and John Wesley's brother Charles Wesley were also significant early leaders in the movement. Early Methodists consisted of all levels of society, including the aristocracy, but the Methodist preachers brought the teachings to laborers and criminals who were likely left outside of organized religion at that time. In Britain, the Methodist Church had a considerable impact in the early decades of the developing working class.

Exercises

I. **Answer the following questions after reading the text.**

　　1. According to the text, why would the author head to the St. Mary's County Oyster Festival and National Shucking Competition?

　　2. How did Thomas Downing eventually become the acclaimed proprietor of Downing's Oyster House?

　　3. Why would Thomas Downing decorate his restaurant with damask curtains, a

chandelier and fine carpeting?

4. What do people usually do at the St. Mary's County Oyster Festival?

5. What is the significance of National Shucking Competition for the people in the town?

II. **Decide whether the following statements are true or false according to the text.**

1. It was the first time that the author had seen oyster shuckers when he attended the St. Mary's County Oyster Festival and National Shucking Competition.

2. Downing's restaurant flourished only because his oysters were better than other restaurants'.

3. The waters where oysters grow in play an important role in the texture of them.

4. At the St. Mary's County Oyster Festival, people can actually enjoy more than just food.

5. For people who lives in Leonardtown, Md., oysters are their first choice when dining in the restaurants.

III. **Fill in the blank of the following sentences with one of the words or phrases given below. Change the form where necessary.**

drift	conjure	suffocate	deplete	tame
straddle	fiddle	pivot	delve	rustic

1. She had forgotten how to _____ up the image of her mother's face.

2. To start figuring out how the virus will transform wildlife of the Americas, researchers have been _____ into the details of how animals pick up the virus.

3. She sold off her equipment and _____ back to her original model of running classes.

4. Villagers were in their colourful headgear huddled together in a lurching _____ truck on a road.

5. The snow had _____ on the ground, swelling up against trunks and rocks, and parchment thin beside the water.

6. While climbing out of the window, his neck got stuck and it appears he was unable to breathe and _____ .

7. It was an exciting experience then, but very _____ compared with today's high-speed jet travel.

8. Feeling strangely out of place, DJ _____ with her fingers in her lap and looked around nervously.

9. The mountains _____ the French-Swiss border.

10. Responding to major _____ of marine fish populations and other wildlife killed in the process of fishing, marine conservation groups became a force in national and international environmental policy.

IV. Translate the following sentences into Chinese.

1. Chincoteague was quiet on this clear blue day in September, but between the succession of seafood shacks and ice-cream parlors I felt the pulse of a town aware of its history. The regional boom in oysters that began in the mid-19th-century still hangs over the place whose nearness to waters that were once rich with oyster reefs allowed the industry to thrive.

2. Oyster farmers have largely replaced oyster tongers, and while raising oysters doesn't replace the wonder that comes with unearthing shells from a wild reef, the practice allows farmers to protect oyster seed from predators, disease and even the simple threat of soft mud, which, given the absence of a hardened reef, could bury and suffocate an oyster.

3. His restaurant flourished. The new dining haven signaled a shift in the way people perceived oysters, both as a food and social experience. It's this complexity in the cultural interpretation of oysters and the way they've been represented over time that fascinates me.

4. The oysters themselves are somewhat blander than the Northeastern fare with their crisp brininess. Since the Gulf of Mexico stays warm throughout the year, Gulf Coast oysters are softer. And since the Mississippi River flushes its freshwater at the foot of the Gulf's estuaries, the salinity of oysters is tame.

5. The moment was moving, but it did make me reflect on how much she'd likely endured or narrowly avoided in this part of Americana, something I could relate to as a black man there from out of town. I stayed wary, but was comfortable that in this

setting, most negative sentiments would be contained.

V. Select one word for each blank from the following word bank. You may not use any of the words in the bank more than once. Change the form where necessary.

challenge	compare	reason	combine	ventilation
desire	predict	customer	vaccinate	warm

As soon as the first snowflakes fell in New York City on Monday, restaurateurs knew what was on the way. Deborah Williamson, the owner of James, in the Prospect Heights area of Brooklyn, said that right now about 50%–70% of her customers are choosing to eat outside. But by January and February, she __1__, "it's going to be a whole different matter."

"I'm kind of prepared for just about anything, and we'll just kind of take it and do the best that we can as we move along. But I do think it's going to be __2__," Ms. Williamson said.

As New York faces its second winter with expanded outdoor dining, a ban on propane heaters has been reinstated by Mayor Bill de Blasio, and the newly discovered Omicron variant is raising concerns about group activities like eating out. Governor Kathy Hochul declared a state of emergency last Friday.

New Yorkers' __3__ for outdoor dining will be tested, said Andrew Rigie, the executive director of the New York City Hospitality Alliance. __4__ with this time last year, he said, there are already fewer people eating outside. One __5__ may be that diners can now eat indoors, unlike last winter, when dining rooms were closed. Still, Mr. Rigie is hopeful that overall, this winter will be better for restaurants.

"Throughout the winter and into the future, outdoor dining is going to be a critically important part of the restaurant industry, both for small business owners and __6__," he said. "This year, with indoor dining being open, it'll be a test to see how customers decide to dine: outdoors versus indoors, or a __7__."

Indoor dining may be safer this year than last year, because guests must present proof of __8__ and about 70% of New Yorkers have been fully vaccinated. But renewed concerns about the spread of the coronavirus — cases, hospitalizations and Covid-related deaths in New York City have risen slightly, with an average of 1,459 new cases a day — could also steer diners to the outdoor seats, where __9__ may be better.

Some restaurants are working to outfit their outdoor-dining structures to make them as __10__ as possible without propane heaters, which are more powerful than electric heaters.

Part III   Extensive Reading

Text B

Fergus Henderson's "Whole Animal" Recipes Inspired Chefs on Both Sides of the Atlantic

It is November 2009 and I'm in a new restaurant on Fairfax Avenue in Los Angeles called Animal. I have been in the city for three weeks, serving as a judge on a TV food contest, all British piss and vinegar to the familiar American gush, and I'm missing my family terribly. No matter, for here on the menu is roast bone marrow with parsley salad, the dish made famous by the chef Fergus Henderson at his Clerkenwell restaurant St. John. His guiding principle:"If you're going to bang an animal on the head it's only polite to eat it all."

I scoop the hot, wobbly jewels of marrow from the bones, pile them on to the toast and add a little salt. Suddenly, I am no longer homesick. A few days later I fly to Chicago and visit another new restaurant. It's called Publican. There it is again: roast bone marrow with parsley salad. "We completely acknowledge that we stole it from Fergus," a chef says to me. "We have, like, three copies of *Nose to Tail Eating* in the kitchen."

The books featured in this series so far have had a serious impact on legions of home cooks. *Nose to Tail Eating: A Kind of British Cooking* written by Fergus Henderson is different. "It was mostly bought by people working in restaurant kitchens," says Georgina Morley, the editor who acquired it for Macmillan, publishers of the original 1999 edition. "The general punter just wasn't particularly interested." It won a prestigious André Simon Award, and received great reviews, but it didn't really sell.

Macmillan eventually handed back the rights and in 2004 Bloomsbury published a new edition, with an adoring introduction by the late Anthony Bourdain, who had become a huge fan of St. John and tight friends with Henderson. In 2007 there was a second volume, *Beyond Nose to Tail*, followed in 2012 by *The Complete Nose to Tail*, which brought the two books together (the edition I have).

Henderson trained as an architect and there has always been something of the art school student about his approach. St. John, housed in a former smokehouse, is a sharp-edged white space. To those used to the velvet plush of ambitious restaurants, its canteen vibe can seem austere. Then there are certain dishes: not just the caveman heft of the bone marrow (which Henderson freely says he picked up from the film *La Grande Bouffe*), but the offer of crispy pig tails to be gnawed upon, or a plate of eggs and carrots.

Likewise, the book does have encouraging food shots: a glistening boiled ham, a bread pudding swamped in butterscotch sauce. But elsewhere there's a shot of a raw pig's head being shaved with a Bic razor, or another of a cook cradling a lamb carcass as if it were a baby. The prose can also read as a provocation. The deep-fried rabbit recipe insists that younger animals are best. "So if you have a friend with a gun, ask them to aim for the smaller bunnies."

The instructions for the pot roast pig's head suggest using only half, "as it is a perfect romantic supper for two. Imagine gazing into the eyes of your loved one over a golden pig's cheek, ear and snout." Yes. Just imagine. What really matters, however, are the recipes for dishes anyone with an appetite will want to eat: for a soupy stew of white beans and smoked bacon or a pig's head and potato pie, for a salad of shredded white cabbage and brown shrimps or a steamed lemon and vanilla syrup sponge.

Henderson denies attempting to provoke. "It's just me being me," he tells me, via email. The book, he says, is "a friendly manual to use at home, to cook for friends and family. It reflects how I have always cooked and thought about food". He advises us not to be afraid of ingredients "otherwise they will misbehave". That wilful anthropomorphizing is part of the joy. The celery salt recipe insists the ingredients sit in the fridge for two days "allowing time for the celeriac and salt to get to know each other". Parsley must be lightly chopped "just enough to discipline it". At the same time, it's light on detail. Duck fat must be administered in "dollops". Herbs come in handfuls. Outside of the baking section, there are no temperatures. Ovens are merely hot or medium. Was Henderson presuming a certain confidence in his readers? "Yes and no," he says. "It's there to help and guide and not be a hindrance."

Paul Kahan, now executive chef of The Publican in Chicago, has got to know and cook with Henderson over the years. He readily admits he opened that restaurant because of the book. "It's hugely influential on me," he says. "It was an eye-opener for a young American cook." Rory Welch, head chef of Träkol in Gateshead, which serves its own take on the St. John pig's head, agrees. "It was one of the first cookbooks I bought. I try to keep it pristine. There's no fuss. It's just robust ingredients properly cooked." Lee Tiernan of Black Axe Mangal, who was once head chef of St. John Bread and Wine, got his copy right at the start of his career. "It's full of excitement and possibility and wonder," he says, simply. Henderson acknowledges the influence on restaurant cooks. "I remember travelling to Australia and chefs saying they were about to give up cooking, but then they read *Nose to Tail Eating* and they were happily back in the kitchen."

It's time for me to cook. From the front section I make a rugged salad of roasted red onions, chargrilled Jerusalem artichokes, olives and peppery leaves dressed with a pokey vinaigrette (proof, I think, that this "kind of" British cooking, requires a knowledge of French basics). I fry fat-clad duck legs until browned, nestle them in a bed of carrots, onions and garlic and pour over the best chicken stock until the legs look like "alligators in a swamp". Two hours in the oven delivers crisp-skinned duck and one of those broths whose depths you could stare into for hours on end.

Finally, I celebrate a dessert I was served at St. John which I regard as one of the best: a plate of golden, still-warm madeleines. "The recipe was just there and happily worked and they just kept coming," Henderson tells me. I conclude I should always have a jug of this batter in the fridge for madeleine emergencies. That's the thing about *Nose to Tail Eating*; it's a book within which you will always find something profoundly comforting.

Total words: 1,224

Total Reading Time: _____ minutes _____ seconds

Vocabulary

marrow *n.* 髓,骨髓；西葫芦

parsley *n.* 西芹；欧芹

bang *v.* 猛敲；砸

scoop *v.* 舀

sharp-edged *adj.* 锋利的；尖锐的

plush *n.* 长毛绒

austere *adj.* 朴素的；无华饰的

glistening *adj.* 辉煌的；成功的

butterscotch *n.* (咸味的)奶油糖果

carcass *n.* (尤指供食用的)畜体

shredded *adj.* 切碎的

wilful *adj.* 任性的；故意的

anthropomorphizing *n.* 赋予人性；拟人化

hindrance *n.* 造成妨碍的事物或人

pristine *adj.* 处于原始状态的；崭新的；清新的

fuss *n.* 大惊小怪,无谓的激动(或忧虑,活动)

robust *adj.* 强健的；强壮的

chargrill *v.* 高温烤炙

madeleine *n.* 玛德琳蛋糕(一种贝壳状重油小蛋糕)

Phrases

piss and vinegar 精力；活力

legions of 众多,大批

be gnawed upon 被啃咬

pokey vinaigrette 油醋汁

Notes

André Simon Award: The UK's only food and drink book award celebrating the very best writing in the English language. André Louis Simon was the charismatic leader of the English wine trade for almost all of the first half of the 20th century, and the grand old man of literate connoisseurship for a further 20 years. In 66 years of authorship, he wrote 104 books. For 33 years he was one of London's leading champagne shippers; for another 33 years active president of the Wine and Food Society. Although he lived in England from the age of 25, he always remained a French citizen. He was both Officier of la Légion d'Honneur and holder of the Order of the British Empire.

Syrup sponge: A sponge cake is a cake which is made with flour, sugar and eggs, but no shortening. The cake is distinctly light and fluffy when it is prepared well. These cakes are also very porous, marked with distinctive holes that make them look rather a lot like sponges. In addition to being served on its own, sponge cake is used as the base for many desserts, since it is a very sturdy, durable cake. Its absorbency makes it ideal for desserts that call for cake soaked in syrup or alcohol, since the cake will soak up the flavor without falling apart.

Exercises

I. Answer the following questions after reading the text.

1. Why is the author no longer homesick after he had meal in Animal?
2. Why is the book *Nose to Tail Eating* so popular among chefs and people?
3. What advice does Henderson give when cooking for friends and family?
4. What might be the reason that Bloomsbury published a new edition of the book *Nose to Tail Eating*?
5. What does the author conclude after the conversation with Henderson?

II. Decide whether the following statements are true or false according to the text.

1. Though *Nose to Tail Eating: A Kind of British Cooking* written by Fergus Henderson didn't won André Simon Award, it received great reviews and really sold well.
2. There are totally three volumes of the book series *Nose to Tail Eating*.
3. What really matters as the instructions for the pot roast pig's head are the recipes for dishes anyone with an appetite will want to eat: for a soupy stew of white beans and smoked bacon or a pig's head and potato pie, for a salad of shredded white cabbage and brown shrimps or a steamed lemon and vanilla syrup sponge.
4. When Henderson travelled to Australia, the chefs there said they were about to give up cooking, but then they read *Nose to Tail Eating* and they were happily back in the kitchen.
5. According to the author, *Nose to Tail Eating* is a book within which people will

always find something profoundly comforting.

III. Fill in the blanks with the words given in the brackets. Change the form where necessary.

1. Her head came up so quickly that she _____ (bang) it on the shelf above her.

2. We had a slice of hot apple pie with a couple of _____ (scoop) of vanilla ice cream.

3. A drab, _____ (austere) society had suddenly been plunged into a more competitive, glamorized world in the 1970s and 1980s.

4. In a small bowl mix the juice of the lime with the fish sauce, sugar and the very finely _____ (shred) lime leaves.

5. You don't accept the possibility that a organization may one day _____ (wilful) misuse this information.

6. Many young children go through periods of being _____ (fuss) eaters and this is a normal part of growing up.

7. The country's political system has continued to be _____ (robust) in spite of its economic problems.

8. Melanie looked tired and there were tears _____ (glisten) on her lashes but her face was serene again.

9. In Bosnia, bloated animal _____ (carcass) are floating in inundated fields.

10. White blood cells are produced by the bone _____ (marrow), the soft spongy centre of bones.

IV. Translate the following sentences into Chinese.

1. It is November 2009 and I'm in a new restaurant on Fairfax Avenue in Los Angeles called Animal. I have been in the city for three weeks, serving as a judge on a TV food contest, all British piss and vinegar to the familiar American gush, and I'm missing my family terribly.

2. I scoop the hot, wobbly jewels of marrow from the bones, pile them on to the toast and add a little salt. Suddenly, I am no longer homesick.

3. To those used to the velvet plush of ambitious restaurants, its canteen vibe can seem austere. Then there are certain dishes: not just the caveman heft of the bone marrow, but the offer of crispy pig tails to be gnawed upon, or a plate of eggs and carrots.

4. I fry fat-clad duck legs until browned, nestle them in a bed of carrots, onions and garlic and pour over the best chicken stock until the legs look like "alligators in a swamp". Two hours in the oven delivers crisp-skinned duck and one of those broths whose depths you could stare into for hours on end.

5. I conclude I should always have a jug of this batter in the fridge for madeleine emergencies. That's the thing about *Nose to Tail Eating*; it's a book within which you will always find something profoundly comforting.

V. Topics for discussion.

1. What qualities should a chef obtain?
2. How would you introduce Chinese food to a foreign friend?

Unit **6** **Travel**

Part I Pre-reading Questions

1. What benefits do you think tourism will bring to people?
2. What impact does the COVID-19 have on tourism?
3. How do you define a good trip?
4. Where is your ideal travelling destination? And why?

Part II Intensive Reading

Text A

Angkor: Asia's Ancient "Hydraulic City"

Angkor Wat attracts millions of visitors every year, but most know little of the intricate and vast water system that fed the empire's rise and demise.

Every April during Khmer New Year celebrations, Sophy Peng, her four siblings and parents make the pilgrimage to Cambodia's most sacred mountain, Phnom Kulen. As the birthplace of the mighty Angkor Empire, fabled Kulen's gentle slopes hold a special place in the hearts of locals.

During religious festivals, Cambodians flock to its peak to be blessed by the same waters used to coronate kings since 802 AD. This was when empire founder Jayavarman II was washed with sacred water and declared a devaraja or God King, marking the start of the Angkor Empire. The empire went on to span much of modern-day Cambodia, Laos, Thailand and Vietnam, and house the world's largest pre-industrial urban hub — the city of Angkor.

To immortalize this sacred spot that sits about 50 km north of Siem Reap city, 1,000 lingas — a phallic symbol incarnation of the Hindu god Shiva — were carved into the riverbed at Kbal Spean, where water flows to the Angkor plains and into the Tonle Sap

Lake. Even today, this water is regarded as sacred, and its power is believed to cure illnesses and bring luck.

"This is a very special place for Cambodians; it's an important part of our history," said Peng. "Every year, my family visit Mount Kulen as part of our Khmer New Year rituals. We bring food donations to leave at the temple and pour water from Kbal Spean on us to bring good luck."

Jayavarman Ⅱ's spiritual blessing marked the start of the Angkor Empire's close relationship with water. However, it wasn't until the capital shifted south to Rolous and then to its final resting place for more than five centuries — Angkor — that master engineers were able to use their skills to create the intricate water system that fed the empire's rise and demise.

"The plains of Angkor are ideal for an empire to flourish," explained Dan Penny, a researcher in the geosciences department at the University of Sydney who has extensively studied Angkor. "There are ample resources, such as good rice soil close to the Tonle Sap Lake. The lake is one of the world's most productive inland fisheries and Angkor is sitting right on the north shore of this enormous food bowl. Angkor grew to become a success on the back of these resources."

In the 1950s and 1960s, French archaeologist Bernard Philippe Groslier used aerial archaeology to reconstruct the layout of Angkor's ancient cities. This revealed its vast reach and the complexity of its water management network and led Groslier to dub Angkor the "Hydraulic City".

Since then, archaeologists have carried out extensive research into the water network and the vital role it played. In 2012, the true extent of the hydraulic system, which spans 1,000 square kilometers, was revealed through airborne laser scanning technology led by archaeologist Dr. Damian Evans, a research fellow at École Française d'Extrême-Orient.

"The missing pieces of the puzzle came into sharp focus," said Dr. Evans. "We're working on a paper now which is the final definitive map of Angkor and shows the real picture, including the hydraulic system. Water was one of the secrets to the empire's success."

To craft a city of its size, the man-made canals carved to steer water from Phnom Kulen to the plains of Angkor were key to construction. They were used to transport the estimated 10 million sandstone bricks, weighing up to 1,500 kg each, that built Angkor.

As well as ensuring a year-round water supply in a monsoon climate to support the population, agriculture and livestock, the hydraulic system feeds the foundations that have kept the temples standing for centuries. The sandy soil alone is not enough to withstand the weight of the stones. However, master engineers discovered mixing sand and water creates stable foundations, so the moats that surround each temple were designed to provide a constant supply of groundwater. This has created foundations strong enough to keep the temples stable and prevent them from crumbling all these centuries later.

Throughout the empire's history, successive kings expanded, restored and improved

Angkor's complex water network. This comprises an impressive web of canals, dykes, moats, barays — the West Baray is the earliest and largest man-made structure that can be spotted from space, at 7.8 km long and 2.1 km wide — as well as master engineering to control water flow.

There are many examples of historic cities with elaborate water management systems, but nothing like this "Angkor's hydraulic system is so unique because of its scale," said Penny. "There are many examples of historic cities with elaborate water management systems, but nothing like this. The scale of the reservoirs, for example. The amount of water the West Baray holds is incredible. Many European cities could have comfortably sat within it when it was built. It's mind-boggling; it's a sea."

However, while it was water that contributed to the Angkor Empire's rise, it was also water that contributed to its demise. "It's clear the water management network was really important in the growth of the city and led to wealth and power," said Penny. "But as it grew more complex and larger and larger, it became the Achilles' heel to the city itself."

Research reveals that in the late 14th and early 15th centuries, dramatic shifts in climate caused prolonged monsoon rains followed by intense droughts. These climate changes took their toll on the water management network, contributing to the mighty empire's eventual fall.

"The whole city was being slapped around by these huge weather variations," said Penny. "The scale of the network and its interdependence meant the massive disturbance of droughts and people changing the system to cope followed by very wet years blew parts apart. This fragmented the whole network, making it unusable."

Further research suggests these weather shifts, combined with the breakdown of the hydraulic system and increasing attacks from the neighbouring Siamese, caused the capital to shift south to Oudong.

"The history books tell you the end of Angkor is because the Siamese overran it in 1431," said Dr. Damian. "I don't think that happened. The evidence we have indicates it was more long-term. The pressure of huge droughts, the water management system breaking down, constant attacks from the Siamese and the expansion of maritime routes all contributed."

Regardless, once Angkor was abandoned, it was reclaimed by nature. While locals were aware of the ancient monuments, they were shrouded by jungle from the rest of the world until 1860, when they were "rediscovered" by French explorer Henri Mouhot. This sparked a series of huge restoration projects that continue today.

In the last two decades, Cambodia has seen a huge increase in tourists flocking to Angkor Wat Archaeological Park to stand in the shadows of Angkor Wat, Ta Prohm and Bayon temples. In 2019, 2.2 million people explored the site. The surge in hotels, eateries and visitors put huge pressure on water demand, causing drastic shortages. As the temples rely on a constant groundwater supply to remain standing, this sparked concern over the preservation of the UNESCO-listed site.

The increase in water demand coupled with severe monsoon flooding from 2009 to

2011, triggered a mass restoration of the ancient water system. Socheata Heng, who owns a guesthouse on the outskirts of Siem Reap, recalled the 2011 floods — the province's worst in 50 years. "It caused so much damage," she said. "Crops were destroyed, communities had to be evacuated and the water came pouring into my guesthouse. It was devastating."

Headed by APSARA National Authority, which is tasked with protecting Angkor Archaeological Park, the restoration project has seen many of the hydraulic system's barays and waterways renovated, including Angkor Thom's 12 km moat, the West Baray and the 10th-century royal basin, Srah Srang. These efforts have helped combat the water shortages triggered by the sharp rise in tourists, and also prevent the severe flooding experienced across the province between 2009 and 2011.

This means today, the vast system that dates back centuries continues to satisfy Siem Reap's thirst by providing a constant water supply, preventing destructive flooding and providing the foundations that will keep Angkor's sacred temples stable well into the future.

"The renovation of the barays and water systems provides water for irrigation, so they have become part of today's agrarian landscape while also helping stabilize the temples," said Dr. Evans. "It's truly incredible this water management system still serves Siem Reap."

Total words: 1,525

Total Reading Time: _____ minutes _____ seconds

💬 Vocabulary

intricate *adj.* 错综复杂的

demise *n.* 终止；失败；死亡

pilgrimage *n.* 朝圣之旅

coronate *v.* 加冕

immortalize *v.* 使不朽；使名垂千古

incarnation *n.* 化身；代表某种品质的人

archaeologist *n.* 考古学家

aerial *adj.* 空中的；空气中的；地表以上的；从飞机上的

hydraulic *adj.* 水力的，液压的；与水利（或液压）系统有关的

steer *v.* 驾驶；操纵，控制；引导

moat *n.* 护城河

dyke *n.* 堤；坝

baray *n.* 人工湖

mind-boggling *adj.* 难以置信的；令人震惊的

shroud *v.* 覆盖；隐藏；隐瞒

devastating *adj.* 毁灭性的；毁灭性的；令人震惊的

agrarian *adj.* 土地的；农业的；耕地的

Phrases

take one's toll 造成损失，造成伤亡

Notes

Achilles' heel: An Achilles' heel (or Achilles heel) is a weakness in spite of overall strength, which can lead to downfall. While the mythological origin refers to a physical vulnerability, idiomatic references to other attributes or qualities that can lead to downfall are common. In Greek mythology, when Achilles was an infant, it was foretold that he would perish at a young age. To prevent his death, his mother Thetis took Achilles to the River Styx, which was supposed to offer powers of invulnerability. She dipped his body into the water but, because she held him by his heel, it was not touched by the water of the river.

UNESCO: The United Nations Educational, Scientific and Cultural Organization is a specialized agency of the United Nations aimed at promoting world peace and security through international cooperation in education, the arts, the sciences, and culture. It has 193 member states and 11 associate members, as well as partners in the non-governmental, intergovernmental, and private sector. It is headquartered at the World Heritage Centre in Paris, France.

APSARA National Authority: APSARA (Authority for the Protection of the Site and Management of the Region of Angkor) is the Cambodian management authority responsible for protecting the Angkor Archaeological Park. Founded in 1995, it is in charge of the research, protection, and conservation as well as the urban and tourist development of the park. It is headquartered in Siem Reap. As of 2016, it consisted of 15 departments and more than 500 personnel.

Exercises

I.　**Answer the following questions after reading the text.**

1. According to the text, what incident indicates the start of the Angkor Empire?
2. What are the reasons for Angkor Empire to flourish?
3. Why would the growth of water management network become the Achilles' heel to the city itself?
4. What difference has the flourishing tourism made to Cambodia in the last two decades?
5. What efforts has APSARA National Authority made to help combat the water shortages triggered by the sharp rise in tourists?

II. Decide whether the following statements are true or false according to the text.

1. The sacred spot that sits about 50 km north of Siem Reap city, 1,000 lingas — a phallic symbol incarnation of the Hindu god Shiva — were carved into the riverbed at Kbal Spean, where water flows to the Angkor plains and into the Tonle Sap Lake. Even today, this water is regarded as wicked, and it is believed to bring illnesses and bad luck.

2. Angkor's hydraulic system is so unique because of its scale. The amount of water is incredible, which is just like sea.

3. The main reason for the mighty empire's eventual fall is dramatic shifts in climate.

4. The vast system that dates back centuries on longer satisfies Siem Reap's thirst by providing a constant water supply. It fails preventing destructive flooding and providing the foundations that will keep Angkor's sacred temples stable into the future.

5. It's extremely incredible that the water management system still serves Siem Reap. The renovation of the barays and water systems provides water for irrigation, so they have become part of today's agrarian landscape while also helping stabilize the temples.

III. Fill in the blank of the following sentences with one of the words or phrases given below. Change the form where necessary.

immortalize	hydraulic	shroud	devastating	incarnation
intricate	aerial	mind-boggling	archaeologist	demise

1. I seem to remember my dreams in unusually _____ detail and twice as often as most people.

2. In February, 1997 a small group of Scottish scientists were forever _____ in genetic advancement history.

3. An American pilot sacrificed his life in an _____ battle with Japanese planes.

4. Mitchell reports that further _____ analysis will be conducted within the next two weeks by the Water Resources Hydrology Department.

5. Tourism is the world's fastest growing industry and the sheer scale of the choices available to punters at the moment is _____ .

6. The whole mountain is _____ by clouds and mist, which the wind blows into various strange shapes.

7. These attacks will _____ industrial cities across the United States which have already seen tens of thousands of manufacturing jobs disappear over the last two decades.

8. The purpose of _____ is to understand the past by studying its material culture.

9. He believed he had been a prince in a previous _____.

10. The _____ of our fishing industry in recent years has resulted in constant high unemployment and emigration from our islands.

IV. Translate the following sentences into Chinese.

1. During religious festivals, Cambodians flock to its peak to be blessed by the same waters used to coronate kings since 802 AD. This was when empire founder Jayavarman Ⅱ was washed with sacred water and declared a devaraja or God King, marking the start of the Angkor Empire.

2. However, it wasn't until the capital shifted south to Rolous and then to its final resting place for more than five centuries — Angkor — that master engineers were able to use their skills to create the intricate water system that fed the empire's rise and demise.

3. Research reveals that in the late 14th and early 15th centuries, dramatic shifts in climate caused prolonged monsoon rains followed by intense droughts. These climate changes took their toll on the water management network, contributing to the mighty empire's eventual fall.

4. Regardless, once Angkor was abandoned, it was reclaimed by nature. While locals were aware of the ancient monuments, they were shrouded by jungle from the rest of the world until 1860, when they were "rediscovered" by French explorer Henri Mouhot.

5. This means today, the vast system that dates back centuries continues to satisfy Siem Reap's thirst by providing a constant water supply, preventing destructive flooding and providing the foundations that will keep Angkor's sacred temples stable well into the future.

V. Select one word for each blank from the following word bank. You may not use any of the words in the bank more than once. Change the form where necessary.

concert	itinerary	flock	protection	close
optimum	recover	eye	anniversary	radar

For years now, I've been asking some of the smartest people in travel about what's on their radar for the coming years. These super-agents know what they're talking about, keeping their ears on their clients' interests, their ___1___ on their own adventures in every corner of the world and their fingers on the pulse of the industry.

But this uncertain year, as I was getting into it, something dawned on me: What's the big rush? This places aren't going to evaporate. If right now doesn't make sense, there will be a time in the coming years when it makes more sense than ever.

I tapped a few of the people I check in with every year. Here's what's on their ___2___.

Bend, Oregon

"Bend is to Oregon, in many ways, what Aspen is to Colorado," says Marchant, "Well-heeled, brimming with vibrant restaurants and shops, enveloped by a veritable outdoor mecca and supported by a talented artistic community. This laid-back, under-the-radar enclave is full of character and host to a steady lineup of seasonal activities, from festivals to ___3___, bike races to brewery hops. But it's the natural world that is truly the draw from fly fishing, mountain biking, hiking, rock climbing, and even explore lava tubes to learn more about what makes the soil of the area so unique." Black Tomato's new trip combines Bend and the Willamette Valley, with lava tube cave expeditions and helicopter tours.

Cambodia and Thailand

"While Thailand officially opened November, we see early 2022 as the ___4___ time to visit," proclaims Ross, who was based in Cambodia for many years. "By then they will be truly open with services available, but the crowds won't have come back en-mass. Cambodia is also opening this month, and the idea of seeing Angkor Wat without the crowds is amazing. I will say, we also want to get travelers back to Southeast Asia to help the drivers, guides and communities on the ground. We can't wait to get travelers back, both to enjoy these countries without the crowds, but also to be a positive part of their regrowth and ___5___!"

Cashel, County Tipperary, Ireland

"Next year marks the 100-year ___6___ of the signing of the Irish Constitution, and along with it, "a new wave of elevated experiences and service are arriving," notes Marchant. "The Rock of Cashel, one of the most spectacular and iconic landmarks in Ireland, is a sight to behold. While the locale has long held an appeal for tourists, it was rarely more than a day trip as part of a larger ___7___. But there really is so much more to see, and this region is brimming with character, from local artisans, family-owned woolen mills and distilleries to one of the finest horse training establishments in the world. Warmth and authenticity radiate from every corner, and with an exciting new Relais & Chateaux hotel opening in the spring of 2022, there is no better time to visit this truly wondrous part of Ireland."

Costa Rica

"Considered to be stable and safe, Costa Rica rebounded quickly from the pandemic and continued to steadily develop this past year in the luxury and adventure segments," explains Cohen. "Six Senses, One & Only and the new Nihi are all set to open in Guanacaste, as are more luxury global hotel brands. Travelers are ___8___ to this 'blue zone', which also happens to be known as one of the happiest countries in the world, to enjoy its microclimates, volcanoes, wildlife, and beaches." But there are still places to see the authentic local flavor of Costa Rica that put it on the map of one of the world's most biodiverse destinations and leader in sustainable travel in the first place. A great new way to access the incredible wildlife of Costa Rica is through the new Boena Wilderness Lodges which is under entirely Costa Rican ownership.

The Galápagos, Ecuador

"After a year of being ___9___, the Galápagos is finally open, and the marine and land wildlife is more prolific than ever!" proclaims Cohen. "One of the most impressive marine landscapes in the world got even better. The president of Ecuador even recently announced at the COP26 Summit in Glasgow the expansion of the Galapagos Marine Reserve by 60,000 square kilometers, which is a very important step for the ___10___ of endangered marine species." Uncharted works with an array of yachts that support conservation efforts and initiatives, the most exciting being the Aqua Mare, the first true small boutique luxury yacht in the Galapagos, with a small carbon footprint and a great guide to guest ratio.

Part III　Extensive Reading

Text B

The Scottish Isle Where Native Ponies Roam

Long only accessible by sea, Eriskay's isolation has protected the Eriskay pony, one of the UK's oldest and rarest breeds and the last remnant of Scotland's native horse.

Strung off the western coast of Scotland and regularly lashed by the North Atlantic, the Western Isles can often feel like a severe and lonely place. On the small Hebridean island of Eriskay, I followed a single road through a stark, treeless landscape dominated by the greys and deep greens of its rocky slopes. To the north, a sparse scattering of sturdy houses were braced against the wind while a stretch of white-sand beach brightened the island's western edge. If Eriskay appeared a rugged place, it was an appearance that seemed to reflect its endurance against hardships wrought by both nature and history.

Eriskay resembles an asterisk at the end of a string of bigger islands: North Uist; Benbecula; and South Uist. Only 2.5 miles long and 1.5 miles wide, Eriskay is the final link in the chain of causeways that tether the islands together, its connection to South Uist completed just 20 years ago. Long accessible only by sea, road access stabilized its then-drastically declining population — islanders can now work or study off-island while still living on Eriskay — and eased travel for visitors. Yet that long isolation had its benefits. It protected such idiosyncratic attractions as the Eriskay Pony, one of the UK's oldest and rarest breeds and the last remnant of Scotland's native horse. As I walked, I spotted a herd grazing high on the hill.

By carrying peat and seaweed on their backs, the small, hardy and docile ponies were once crucial to croft work. Every island family used to have a pony, said Sandra MacInnes, secretary of Comann Each nan Eilean (Eriskay Pony Society). "They wouldn't have survived without the pony. They wouldn't have got peat to keep them warm, they wouldn't have got seaweed to help the crops."

But by the 1970s, largely due to cross breeding and the rise in use of motor vehicles for transportation and work, they'd come close to extinction. While a number of pure mares survived, there was only one pure-bred stallion, named Eric, left. Founded in 1972, the society helped bring the breed back from the brink. While still categorized as critically endangered, there are now 300 in the UK, all descended from Eric.

The formation of the pony society occurred at a time of increasing cultural awareness and confidence in Scotland. The Scottish National Party (SNP) gained its first MP in 1967, and the ponies may have been a beneficiary of the more assured national mood. In his research into the pony society's formation, Liam Crouse, PhD researcher at Sabhal Mòr Ostaig UHI college, learned that its early membership "included some notable SNP members, as well as some of the Gaelic intelligentsia at a national level". He said he's "trying to piece together the impetuses of the instigation of the society in 1972, but I think it is a combination of an increasingly confident Scottish cultural society and the realization in Eriskay that these ponies were both unique and rare."

The revival of Eriskay's ponies is just one part of the island's reclamation of its history. For years, Eriskay was better known for what had arrived on its shores than for its own rich heritage.

Home to around 130 majority Catholic and Gaelic-speaking residents, Eriskay may be small but it has found itself at the centre of several dramatic events. It was on Eriskay's stretch of silvery sand, now known as Coilleag a' Phrionnsa, or "the Prince's Cockle Strand", that in 1745 Charles Edward Stuart (better-known as Bonnie Prince Charlie) first set foot in Scotland to launch his doomed Jacobite uprising to retake the British throne. The consequences, following defeat the next year at the Battle of Culloden, were disastrous for the Highlands and Islands. Britain terrorized them through indiscriminate killing; dismantled social structures by breaking up clans; and attempted to erase cultural identity through banning the wearing of tartan and suppressing the use of Gaelic.

The second event that has long defined the island occurred in 1941, when the SS Politician, carrying some 22,000 cases of fine malt whisky in its hold, struck submerged sandbanks off Eriskay. Having first helped to rescue the crew, the islanders soon set about liberating the whisky in the belief that the cargo was theirs under the "rules of salvage". UK Customs and Excise took a different view. Islanders' homes were raided and several were tried for illegal salvaging, smuggling and black market selling of goods and sentenced to prison. Despite this dark end to the story, and islanders' lingering sense of injustice, writer Compton Mackenzie spun the tale into *Whisky Galore!*, a novel later made into a comedy film.

Today, Eriskay's lone pub, Am Politician, embraces the history. It's decorated with photos of the SS Politician and has a handful of salvaged, still unopened whisky bottles tucked behind the bar.

Visiting such celebrated sites as the pub and the prince's beach is easier now that there's road access to Eriskay. Travellers can just pop over for a few hours, check them off, then turn back north towards the Outer Hebrides. But in recent years, islanders have been working on ways to entice visitors to stay longer.

I had travelled the old, slow way, coming north by sea from the Island of Barra, and chose to stay a while, booking a few nights at the Oir na Mara bed and breakfast. With plenty of time to fill, I set out to walk around the coastline. At several particularly scenic spots I came across laminated pages of poetry tucked into boxes. They seemed to make up a curious scavenger hunt scattered across the island. Titled Maighstir Ailein's Poetry Trail, each page featured verses in Gaelic and English from Eilein na h-Òige (Isle of Youth) written at the turn of the 20th century by Father Allan MacDonald, whose careful documentation of the Gaelic oral tradition — the songs, poems and folk tales that made up a vibrant cultural heritage then on the verge of disappearing — helped to rescue it from oblivion.

The poetry trail had been put together by Comann Eachdraidh Eirisgeidh (the Eriskay Historical Society). The society was established in 2010 to collect and preserve materials of historical value to the island, something that hadn't been done much before. "When you're growing up in a community, you perhaps don't give it credit for how distinctive that community is," said Iain Ruaraidh, the society's chairperson. Initiatives such as the poetry trail encourage a deeper exploration of Eriskay's heritage, and the society recently purchased the island's school, closed since 2013, to turn it into a heritage centre where visitors can learn more — it's currently one of the few islands in the Outer Hebrides that lacks one.

Later, at the B&B, I asked where it might be possible to see the ponies up-close, as I'd been under the impression that they wandered wild across the island. Without hesitation, the owner Iagan drove me to see some of his. I was only half mistaken: the ponies spend the summer grazing on the hill of Beinn Sciathan to allow crops to grow in the settlements, but they spend their winters roaming freely in the township. As I petted the ponies, Iagan told me that he wished more people were interested in them so they could rebound further. Thanks to the pony society, which has stepped up promotion of the breed in recent years, he may soon get his wish.

The historical society plans to promote the breed in the new heritage centre, too. "We're trying to get people more aware of the Eriskay ponies and get them into breeding themselves and using them throughout the islands and on the mainland," said MacInnes. "We're also going to teach traditional skills like making creels and taking the ponies down to the beach for seaweed." It's all part of embracing Eriskay's heritage and reclaiming what makes this island so unique, and, she said, "going back to the traditional skills to show people how it was".

Total words: 1,462

Total Reading Time: _____ minutes _____ seconds

💬 **Vocabulary**

remnant *n.* 剩余部分

lash *v.* 鞭打；猛击；捆扎

stark *adj.* 粗陋的；严酷的；荒凉的

sparse *adj.* 稀疏的；稀少的

sturdy *adj.* 结实的；坚固的；强健的；坚定的

asterisk *n.* 星号；星状物

idiosyncratic *adj.* 乖僻的；怪异的

graze *v.* 吃草；放牧

croft *n.*（尤指苏格兰的）家庭小农场佃户，家庭小农场主

pure-bred *adj.* 纯种的

brink *n.* 边缘；初始状态

impetus *n.* 促进；动力；惯性

instigation *n.* 发起；唆使；煽动

dismantle *v.* 拆开，拆卸；废除，取消

tartan *n.*（尤指苏格兰织物的）花格图案；方格花纹

submerged *adj.* 在水中的；淹没的；水下的

salvage *v.* 打捞；抢救；营救

roam *v.* 徜徉，漫步

laminated *adj.* 粘合的；层压的

scavenger *n.* 拾荒者；捡破烂的人

creel *n.*（钓鱼用的）鱼篓

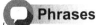

Phrases

string off 呈串（排列）
brace against 支撑，撑牢

Notes

Scottish National Party: The Scottish National Party (SNP) is a Scottish nationalist and social democratic political party in Scotland. The SNP supports and campaigns for Scottish independence from the United Kingdom and for membership of the European Union, with a platform based on civic nationalism. The SNP is the largest political party in Scotland, where it has the most seats in the Scottish Parliament and 45 out of the 59 Scottish seats in the House of Commons at Westminster, and it is the third-largest political party by membership in the United Kingdom, behind the Labour Party and the Conservative Party. The current Scottish National Party leader, Nicola Sturgeon, has served as First Minister of Scotland since 20 November, 2014.

Uist: the Uists are the central group of islands in the Outer Hebrides of Scotland. North Uist and South Uist are linked by causeways running via Benbecula and Grimsay, and the entire group is sometimes known as the Uists.

Exercises

I. **Answer the following questions after reading the text.**

1. What contributes to the pure-bred ponies on Eriskay?

2. Why does Eriskay appear like a rugged place?

3. Why would Eriskay pony come close to extinction by the 1970s?

4. How did the pony society eventually form?

5. What does the historical society plan to do to promote the breed in the new heritage centre?

II. **Decide whether the following statements are true or false according to the text.**

1. The long isolation brought no benefits to Eriskay.

2. Eriskay may be small but it has found itself at the centre of several dramatic events.

3. It's getting easier to visit the celebrated sites as the pub and the prince's beach. Travellers can just pop over for a few hours, check them off, then turn back north towards the Outer Hebrides. Recently, islanders have been working on ways to entice visitors to stay longer.

4. The ponies spend the winters grazing on the hill of Beinn Sciathan to allow crops

to grow in the settlements, but they spend their summers roaming freely in the township.

5. Iagan wished more people were interested in ponies so they could rebound further.

III. Fill in the blanks with the words given in the brackets. Change the form where necessary.

1. Outside of this relatively unchanged _____ (remnantal) of the old way of life, Algerian cities are a mix of Western influence and Arabic tradition.

2. The acting is pointed, the action is brutal, and the tale is _____ (sparse) told.

3. The United States is on the _____ (brink) of a crisis in health care, particularly for hospitals.

4. An appeal fund was launched at the _____ (instigation) of the President.

5. It is likely the tower will be _____ (dismantle) piece by piece using a large crane and a scaffold to support the remaining structure.

6. Crews in Central Texas pulled this woman to safety after fast-moving waters swept and _____ (submerge) her car.

7. Anywhere he _____ (roam), she is there, a reminder of the fragility of his heart and of his sham relationships.

8. Butter is _____ (laminate) between layers of dough and both must have the same consistency.

9. The leather is supple and _____ (sturdy) enough to last for years.

10. The expanded literature search was very coincident with the initial search, providing most of the same reasons, purposes, and _____ (impetus) for developing peer institution selection systems.

IV. Translate the following sentences into Chinese.

1. Strung off the western coast of Scotland and regularly lashed by the North Atlantic, the Western Isles can often feel like a severe and lonely place. On the small Hebridean island of Eriskay, I followed a single road through a stark, treeless landscape dominated by the greys and deep greens of its rocky slopes.

2. Long accessible only by sea, road access stabilized its then-drastically declining population — islanders can now work or study off-island while still living on Eriskay — and eased travel for visitors.

3. Home to around 130 majority Catholic and Gaelic-speaking residents, Eriskay

may be small but it has found itself at the centre of several dramatic events. It was on Eriskay's stretch of silvery sand, now known as Coilleag a' Phrionnsa, or "the Prince's Cockle Strand", that in 1745 Charles Edward Stuart (better-known as Bonnie Prince Charlie) first set foot in Scotland to launch his doomed Jacobite uprising to retake the British throne.

4. I was only half mistaken: the ponies spend the summer grazing on the hill of Beinn Sciathan to allow crops to grow in the settlements, but they spend their winters roaming freely in the township.

5. "We're also going to teach traditional skills like making creels and taking the ponies down to the beach for seaweed." It's all part of embracing Eriskay's heritage and reclaiming what makes this island so unique, and, she said, "going back to the traditional skills to show people how it was".

V. Topics for discussion.

1. How do you think we should balance the development of tourism and the protection of the environment?

2. Please describe in detail what your ideal trip would be like.

7 Marriage and Family

1. What factors should be considered when getting married?
2. What do you think is the secret to a happy marriage?
3. Is child a necessity for a family?
4. Supposing you get married, how are you going to solve the problems appearing in your marriage?

Part II Intensive Reading

Text A

The Secret to a Fight-Free Relationship
(Abridged)

Conventional wisdom says that venting is cathartic and that we should never go to bed angry. But couples who save disagreements for scheduled meetings show the benefits of a more patient approach to conflict.

For decades, when Liz Cutler's husband, Tom Kreutz, did something that bothered her, Cutler would sometimes pull out a scrap of paper from the back of her desk drawer. On it she would scribble down her grievances: maybe Kreutz had stayed late at work without giving her a heads-up, or maybe he'd allowed their kids to do something she considered risky. The list was Cutler's way of honoring a promise she and her husband had made. They would talk about their frustrations only in scheduled meetings — which they held once a year for a time, and later, every three months. It's a system they've adhered to for more than 40 years.

Any psychologist will tell you that conflict is both an inevitable and a vital part of a close relationship. The challenge — which can make the difference between a lasting, satisfying partnership and one that combusts — is figuring out how to manage conflict constructively.

Conventional wisdom treats the passage of time as an adversary. We're told not to "bottle up" hard feelings, let annoyance fester, or go to bed angry. Stockpiling grievances, many therapists warn, invites resentment and sets the stage for partners to erupt.

Cutler and Kreutz, and other partners who have systems of scheduled disagreement, have discovered that delaying hard conversations has the potential to fortify, not corrode, relationships. For them, preplanned meetings in which both parties are prepared for difficult discussions drain some of the most painful emotions from conflict. Partners are then able to focus on solving problems and to do so cooperatively and creatively — sometimes even finding delight in the process. Researchers and clinicians have also come to discover what Cutler and Kreutz figured out on their own — that when tackling challenges in relationships, having a little distance and a recurring calendar invite can help.

The first time Cutler and Kreutz spoke, she was standing behind him in a cafeteria at Duke University in 1974. She tapped him on the shoulder and asked, "Hey, how come sometimes you're so nice, and sometimes you're such a jerk?"

Taken aback, Kreutz said, "I don't even know you."

The two walked through the cafeteria, trays in hand, arguing. Cutler was convinced that Kreutz was the guy with whom she'd spent an entire night dancing — and who sometimes acted as if he didn't know her when she saw him on campus. Over dinner, this argument shifted into a debate about the opposing moral principles of Cutler's Judaism and Kreutz's Catholicism. A few days later, they continued that debate for five hours while perched in the branches of a camellia tree.

"I remember sitting in that tree and just falling in love right there," Kreutz told me. He marveled at all that Cutler had done: ballet, karate, camping, canoeing, climbing. Cutler felt that she had met her match. It was hard to find something Kreutz couldn't do: One day, she'd learn that he knew how to scuba dive; another, she'd discover that he put his climbing skills to use by scaling the side of Duke's chapel. Kreutz even took it upon himself to learn things that she cared about, like teaching himself Hebrew while working on a factory line one summer.

The new couple became known for their inseparability. Even when Cutler walked on campus by herself, people would call out, "Hi, Liz and Tom!"

They were equally well known for their operatic conflicts. "Our friends couldn't stand it," Cutler recalled, "because we would escalate to the point where one of us would get in the car and drive away." Once, Kreutz put his fist through a wall.

"Showing anger in dramatic ways was clearly part of our back-and-forth," Kreutz said.

When Cutler studied abroad during her junior year, they kept in touch through pay phones and letters written on wispy blue aerogram papers. But when she returned to Duke, after spending nine months on her own, Cutler felt stifled by Kreutz's desire to be with her constantly. She didn't want to lose him, but she didn't want to be "swallowed up" by the relationship. They decided to make a contract: They would stay together for another year, and as part of that agreement, they'd try to resolve what wasn't working well, including their frequent fights and insufficient boundaries. When the year was up, they would determine whether to continue the relationship.

This conversation, in which they spent a full day wandering around Duke's campus hashing things out, brought the couple a sense of relief. They each had their say and felt the other took their concerns seriously. When they hit the one-year mark, they agreed to continue the relationship for another year — and to re-up the contract discussion. Soon it became an annual event, which they dubbed "contract talks". About a decade later, they realized that a year was long enough for their problems to calcify, so they made their contract talks quarterly affairs.

They set norms governing the space, time, and tone for their discussions. They'd escape to somewhere quiet and pleasant — a path where they could take a long walk, or occasionally the house in Michigan where Cutler had spent summers as a kid. They established "rules of engagement". Among them: Don't shut down the other person's observations. If one person says that something is a problem for the relationship — even if the other person doesn't think it's important — it's a problem. Prepare to hear criticism, admit your faults, and be grateful for your partner. Commit to working on the relationship for the long haul, and accept that change might come in baby steps.

By their late 30s, Cutler and Kreutz were reserving most of their problem-solving for contract talks. With those talks scheduled, they didn't feel compelled to raise issues in the moment. And they noticed that by waiting, they could avoid the pain and gamesmanship of impulsive arguments; in the midst of a fight, they were too preoccupied with "winning" to attempt to solve problems. For Cutler, the distance often brought clarity. By the time she had read through the paper in her desk drawer to prepare for an upcoming contract talk, she would deem some of the entries too trivial to raise. Their "rules of engagement" specified that they had to be "in an emotionally calm state" — a stipulation that the two say they've found easy to follow. The pause between the initial frustration and the discussion, Cutler told me, "gives you time to put your little ego to bed and to be the grown-up, and not the child inside you."

Once the couple had kids, both the substance and structure of their talks changed. They added on family contract talks to give their boys a space to speak openly with them. Their two oldest sons went on to voluntarily conduct "brother contract talks" with each other.

The support structure of contract talks began to take on new significance for the family when their youngest son, Isaac, was two and a half. Isaac had several strokes, was in a coma, and was diagnosed with cancer. Cutler remembers that a social worker cautioned her and Kreutz that their relationship might be tested by the stress of seeing their son in pain and round-the-clock caregiving. They were told that the majority of couples who have a child as ill as Isaac break up.

Twenty-four years later, Cutler and Kreutz are still together. "Do I think contract talks saved us?" Cutler said. "Absolutely."

James Córdova, a psychology professor at Clark University, wants people to treat relationships the way they treat their teeth. People don't only go to the dentist when they have a toothache; they get preventive treatment to remove the buildup of plaque and tartar that causes tooth decay. By contrast, many partners seek help only when their problems are so acute that the relationship is irreparably damaged. At that stage, couples receive the equivalent of emergency-room treatment.

Córdova believes that, as with teeth, "inside intimate relationships, there is also a naturally occurring corrosive process." We hurt each other. And when we're hurt, we tend to do one of two things: We hurt our partner back or withdraw. "Neither one of those natural instincts is particularly conducive to long-term intimate health," Córdova told me.

We can hurt one another when disagreements shove the regions of our brain that are responsible for rational thinking into the back seat. When we react without taking time to cool off, we might sting our partner to score points or defend ourselves. And, chances are, that behavior won't bring a feeling of catharsis. At best, venting may provide a temporary mood boost — but in many cases it doesn't accomplish even that. In a seminal psychology study, participants who sat quietly right after their anger was provoked became less angry than those who were instructed to vent.

Instead of treating anger as steam that needs to be released, we seem to be better off running out the clock on it. Research points to the value of taking a time-out — specifically in order to "pause and calm down, not pause and reload". When people use the time-out to take an impartial view of the incident or even distract themselves — rather than stew in their frustration — their anger tends to subside, and they're less likely to try to punish the other person. The mindset that both parties have when they reconvene matters too. Morton Deutsch, a prominent conflict-resolution expert, explains that partners can have constructive disagreement if they foster a mindset focused on learning rather than winning, reframe conflict as a mutual problem to be solved jointly, and set norms of cooperation.

Two decades ago, Córdova designed a process that threads together these insights. He describes it as the marital-health equivalent of the six-month dental visit or annual physical. Over two sessions, the "Marriage Checkup" helps couples assess their strengths and weaknesses. In randomized controlled trials on a variety of populations, Córdova and his team have consistently found that partners who use the Marriage Checkup report improved marital satisfaction and intimacy as well as other important indicators of relationship health.

Unlike Cutler and Kreutz's contract talks, the Marriage Checkup is conducted by a trained third party. It also doesn't encourage partners to confine all conflict to these sessions. The clinicians I spoke with said they wouldn't recommend that most couples wait months to discuss every relationship problem. Urgent issues or small annoyances that can easily be fixed, they explained, are generally worth raising relatively quickly, though it's still worth waiting a few hours or even days for heightened emotions to dissipate. Partners can address bigger issues — such as a change in expectations in the relationship — weeks down the line, or longer. But, they said, if more spaced-out discussions such as contract talks work for a couple, nothing's wrong with that.

Córdova says that what the Marriage Checkup shares with contract talks is its fundamental premise that partners need regular, scheduled times to tend to the knots in their relationship. This can help people like Cutler and Kreutz, whose propensity for heated fights might prevent them from having clearheaded, productive conversations about their disagreements.

Total words: 2,050

Total Reading Time: _____ minutes _____ seconds

💬 **Vocabulary**

scrap *n.* 小块(纸、织物等)

combust *v.* 开始燃烧;开始烧

adversary *n.* 敌手,对手

fester *v.* 溃烂;化脓;愈益恶化

resentment *n.* 愤恨,怨恨

fortify *v.* 加强;增强;强化

corrode *v.* 腐蚀;侵蚀

drain *v.* 喝光,耗尽;排干

recurring *adj.* 循环的

perch *v.* 停留;栖息;坐

karate *n.* 空手道

canoeing *n.* 皮划艇运动(或比赛)

escalate *v.* (使)逐步扩大;不断恶化

wispy *adj.* 一绺绺的;成束的;纤细的

aerogram *n.* 航空邮简(一张薄纸折成,作航空信寄出)

stifle *v.* 压制;扼杀;阻止

calcify *v.* (使)钙化;骨化

gamesmanship *n.* 比赛策略

deem *v.* 认为,视为;相信

round-the-clock *adj.* 全天的,全天候的,不分昼夜的,连续不停的

tartar *n.* 牙石;牙垢

catharsis *n.* 宣泄,净化

time-out *n.* 暂停,休息时间

dissipate *v.* 驱散

Phrases

scribble down 草草记下；匆匆书写

taken aback 惊讶；大吃一惊

marvel at 对……惊奇，惊叹于

scuba dive 潜水；水肺潜水

pay phone 投币式公用电话

hash out 消除，经过长时间讨论解决一个问题

long haul 长途；长距运输；努力得到的结果

in a coma 陷入昏迷

Notes

The Atlantic: Formerly *The Atlantic Monthly*, American journal of news, literature, and opinion founded in 1857 and is one of the oldest and most-respected magazines in the United States. Formerly a monthly publication, it now releases 10 issues a year and maintains an online site. Its offices are in Washington, D.C.

The Marriage Checkup: The book is designed to help couples assess the strengths and weaknesses of their relationship and to develop strategies for strengthening its health. Like physical health, the health of a relationship can be developed to greater levels of fitness and resilience to illness. Thus, even healthy couples can benefit from a marital health perspective by developing exercises for optimizing their health and fitness. This book primarily serves couples interested in improving the health of their relationship. Counselors and therapists may recommend that their couples-patients use the book. Additionally, the book may be of interest to professors of marriage and family counseling.

Exercises

I. **Answer the following questions after reading the text.**

1. What is the system that Liz Cutler and Tom Kreutz adhered to for more than 40 years to deal with the problems appearing in marriage?

2. What difference have those partners who have systems of scheduled disagreement discovered compared with conventional wisdom?

3. Why would people call out "Hi, Liz and Tom!" when Cutler walked on campus by herself?

4. According to the seminal psychology study, instead of treating anger as steam that needs to be released, how should we deal with anger more wisely and efficiently?

5. What "Marriage Checkup" can do to help couples prolong a healthy relationship?

II. Decide whether the following statements are true or false according to the text.

1. Conflict is an inevitable and a vital part of a close relationship. The challenge — which can make the difference between a lasting, satisfying partnership and one that combusts — is figuring out how to manage conflict constructively.

2. Without contract talks, the relationship between Cutler and Kreutz would never go this far.

3. According to the study, participants who sat quietly right after their anger was provoked became angrier than those who were instructed to vent.

4. The "rules of engagement" specified that Cutler and Kreutz had to be "in an emotionally calm state" because the pause between the initial frustration and the discussion gives one time to put little ego to bed and to be the grown-up but not the child inside you.

5. The difference between Cutler and Kreutz's contract talks and the Marriage Checkup is that the latter is conducted by a trained third party.

III. Fill in the blank of the following sentences with one of the words or phrases given below. Change the form where necessary.

resentment	drain	escalate	around the clock	dissipate
combust	fortify	deem	catharsis	corrode

1. The title comes from an image of a moth so in love with a flame that it keeps flinging itself into a candle until it _____ .

2. There is much poverty and anguish in the world, and it breeds _____ and envy.

3. After this brief meeting, we were _____ with some basic knowledge about our surroundings, and we were able to forge ahead to explore on our own.

4. A section of the Leeds and Liverpool canal will have to be _____ in November to allow further work on the construction of Ferncliffe Road bridge.

5. While costs were _____ all the time, we felt that the project would never be completed if we did not push ahead with the work.

6. As the series was _____ a runaway success, it was immediately commissioned again.

7. For the last four days, a team of more than 400 workers has operated _____ to ready the city for its big night.

8. At the end of the movie, an ensemble comedy, there are about half a dozen _____ in a two-minute span of time.

9. Rage suddenly takes control as the other emotions _____ when he'd been pulled

from his meal.

10. His armor had protected him from the poison, though the acidic mix had _____ the metal in several places.

IV. Translate the following sentences into Chinese.

1. Any psychologist will tell you that conflict is both an inevitable and a vital part of a close relationship. The challenge — which can make the difference between a lasting, satisfying partnership and one that combusts — is figuring out how to manage conflict constructively.

2. Conventional wisdom treats the passage of time as an adversary. We're told not to "bottle up" hard feelings, let annoyance fester, or go to bed angry. Stockpiling grievances, many therapists warn, invites resentment and sets the stage for partners to erupt.

3. If one person says that something is a problem for the relationship — even if the other person doesn't think it's important — it's a problem. Prepare to hear criticism, admit your faults, and be grateful for your partner. Commit to working on the relationship for the long haul, and accept that change might come in baby steps.

4. By contrast, many partners seek help only when their problems are so acute that the relationship is irreparably damaged. At that stage, couples receive the equivalent of emergency-room treatment.

5. We can hurt one another when disagreements shove the regions of our brain that are responsible for rational thinking into the back seat. When we react without taking time to cool off, we might sting our partner to score points or defend ourselves.

V. Select one word for each blank from the following word bank. You may not use any of the words in the bank more than once. Change the form where necessary.

contained	inflame	distract	unsure	isolate
string	tension	fragile	correlate	drop-in

It's useful in relationships in which people — such as business partners Erica Cerulo and Claire Mazur — hide from conflict. Besides being close friends, Cerulo and Mazur have a relationship that can be summed up in a __1__ of words with the prefix *co-*: They've been co-owners of a business, co-authors of the book *Work Wife*, and co-hosts of a podcast. After they sold their start-up to a larger company, they used their newfound resources to hire the management coach Ben Michaelis. Michaelis, who's also a clinical psychologist, quickly noticed that, like many people, they tended to avoid conflict. He said they needed to figure out how to deal with disagreement or the __2__ would break their partnership. Cerulo and Mazur had sensed that this avoidance made their partnership feel __3__ and slowed them down when it came to solving problems for their business. They lived in fear that one fight would wreck everything. Michaelis told them to start by vocalizing low-stakes gripes. It was exposure therapy for the conflict-averse.

In time, Cerulo and Mazur were able to tackle thornier issues that could breed resentment if left unaddressed — questions of who's in charge, who is respected more by their team, who gets to do more exciting work. Their weekly drive to their parent company turned out to be an ideal environment in which to talk about these topics. The Brooklyn-to-New Jersey trip was a regular event, which removed the dread of finding a time to discuss a tough subject; the length of the drive set a time limit on the conversation; and sitting side by side meant they didn't have to look each other in the eye. For Cerulo and Mazur, these were ripe conditions for practicing what Michaelis calls "__4__ disagreement".

On one car ride — during a trip in California — Mazur opened up about a source of anxiety for her. She and Cerulo had recently had a business meeting with a woman who'd brought her child along at the last minute. The kid was __5__, and Cerulo complained that they should have rescheduled. These comments about a working parent __6__ a sensitive subject for Mazur. She thought she might want to have kids and knew Cerulo didn't. Part of what made Mazur __7__ about parenthood was her concern about how having children would affect her partnership and friendship with Cerulo. On their drive, Mazur explained what had been going on in her head. Cerulo told Mazur she was looking forward to being part of her kids' lives one day, and shared her own __8__ insecurity: that people in their social circle were becoming parents, and Cerulo worried about being __9__. In that conversation and others, they planned for how to make space in their partnership and friendship for parenthood. When Mazur eventually did have a child and went on maternity leave, Cerulo visited her twice a week. Those ___10___ allowed Mazur to keep up to speed on their company, and Cerulo got to witness her friend's life as a new parent.

Part III　Extensive Reading

Text B

If Bill and Melinda Gates Can't Make a Marriage Work, What Hope Is There for the Rest of Us?

Just imagine how many hours of couples therapy you can afford when you're among the world's richest people. Or the shared sense of purpose you could forge while raising three children and running a $50 billion charitable foundation with your spouse.

Then imagine that it's not enough to keep you together.

In announcing their decision to divorce, Bill and Melinda Gates cited the work they'd done on their marriage, and a mutual sense of pride in their children and philanthropy. But, they said in identical joint statements shared on Twitter, "we no longer believe we can grow together as a couple in this next phase of our lives."

Yes, money is one of the main things couples fight about. But having so much of it that you can give billions away doesn't eliminate the questions that every couple faces: Do we still want similar things in life? Can we still create that life together? Or would it be better if we forged ahead on our own?

This is one of the reasons we regular folks are fascinated when billionaires split. It's comforting to know that relationships are difficult no matter who we are.

"They're real people. They're not above it all. You still have to deal with each other on a human level," says Carlos Lastra, a partner in the family law practice at the Maryland firm Paley Rothman. "They somehow figured out what worked in their relationship for the past 27 years. They couldn't figure out what would work for another 27 years. It doesn't matter what your background is: You've got to figure out your own secret sauce and keep working at it."

Bill and Melinda met at Microsoft in 1987, when he was the company co-founder and she was an employee who grabbed a seat next to him at a work dinner. When he asked her out the first time, she rejected him, saying his date invite "wasn't spontaneous enough", Melinda writes in her 2019 memoir *The Moment of Lift*. Two hours later, he called and asked if she would meet him that evening. "Is this spontaneous enough for you?" he asked.

By those early accounts, their relationship reads like two equals finding their match. "We found we had a lot in common. We both love puzzles and we both love to compete," Melinda writes, noting that he seemed intrigued when she beat him at a math game and at the board game Clue. When they got engaged and someone asked Bill how Melinda made him feel, he answered: "Amazingly, she makes me feel like getting married."

Clearly, a lot has changed since then.

When Jeff and MacKenzie Bezos announced their intention to split in 2019, divorce lawyer Nicole Sodoma highlighted this universal challenge in staying together long-term. "The people we marry are not the people we divorce," she said, "because people change."

For many couples, the pandemic has made it impossible to ignore those shifts. The big pause of the past year kept couples home together for longer hours, canceled work travel and created new roles and routines unexpectedly, Sodoma says, forcing couples who were ignoring problems in their marriages to suddenly face them head-on. From April 2020 to this past month, Sodoma says, her family law practice in Charlotte has seen a 20% increase in requests for consults.

She also thinks that, because the pandemic made many of us grasp life's fragility, there's "more permission to be authentic now than there ever has been". And sometimes that return to our true selves spurs big changes.

Among his clients, Lastra has seen two distinct outcomes for couples who were pondering a split during the pandemic: Stronger than before, or no desire to see each other again.

Another way that Bill, who's 65, and Melinda, who's 56, are just a normal couple? As the stigma surrounding divorce has eroded, the divorce rate for Americans 50 and older has doubled since the 1990s. Jeff and MacKenzie Bezos were 55 and 49, respectively, when they divorced. Al and Tipper Gore split while in their 60s.

Vicki Larson, who's written extensively on divorce and is working on a book about aging as a woman, says that when couples have raised their children to adulthood — the Gateses' are 18 to 25 — they often feel their job as parents is essentially "done," prompting them to reassess their lives. "You go through phases in your marriage and you go through phases as a person, and sometimes they don't jibe," Larson notes. "When you have kids, you're on a path together." Once they're grown, you have to figure out what your shared path will be, Larson adds, or decide this isn't what you want anymore.

"We have a lot of scripts when we're young for how life should look," Larson says, adding that "there's no script for midlife. You get to create it on your own. That's both liberating and scary."

Total words: 901

Total Reading Time: _____ minutes _____ seconds

Vocabulary

forge *v.* 锻造，制作；努力加强

spontaneous *adj.* 自发的，自然的；非勉强的

head-o*n adj.* 正面相撞的

ponder *v.* 沉思；考虑；琢磨

stigma *n.* 耻辱；羞耻

erode *v.* 侵蚀，腐蚀；风化

jibe *v.* 与……一致，与……相符；相匹配

Phrases

forge ahead 迅速向前；进步神速

above it all 超越一切

Notes

Melinda Gates: Née Melinda Ann French, (born on August 15, 1964, Dallas, Texas, U.S.), American businesswoman and philanthropist who — with her then husband, Microsoft Corporation cofounder Bill Gates — founded the charitable Bill & Melinda Gates Foundation.

Jeff Bezos: Jeffrey Preston Bezos (born on January 12, 1964) is an American internet entrepreneur, industrialist, media proprietor, and investor. He is known for the founder and CEO of the multi-national technology company Amazon.

Exercises

I.　**Answer the following questions after reading the text.**

　　1. Why did Bill Gates and Melinda choose to divorce?

　　2. Why are regular folks fascinated when billionaires split?

　　3. How did Bill and Melinda meet at the beginning?

　　4. What impact has the pandemic had on conjugal relationship?

　　5. What is Vicki Larson's opinion on midlife?

II.　**Decide whether the following statements are true or false according to the text.**

　　1. When Bill asked Melinda out the first time, she rejected him because she thought it was not formal enough.

　　2. By those early accounts, the Gates found that they had a lot in common. They both

love puzzles and love to compete, which made them feel like getting married even they just got engaged.

3. For many couples, the pandemic has made it impossible to ignore those shifts. The big pause of the past year kept couples home together for longer hours, canceled work travel and created new roles and routines unexpectedly. Thus, it contributed a 10% increase in requests for family law practice consults.

4. There have been two distinct outcomes for couples who were pondering a split during the pandemic according to Lastra: Stronger than before, or no desire to see each other again.

5. Vicki Larson, who's written extensively on divorce and is working on a book about aging as a woman, says that when couples have raised their children to adulthood they often feel their job as parents is essentially "done", prompting them to reassess their lives. "You go through phases in your marriage and you go through phases as a person, and sometimes they don't jibe."

III. Fill in the blanks with the words given in the brackets. Change the form where necessary.

1. In the former case, the figure's head was chopped off and posted as a trophy, and the remaining metal was _____ (forge) into bullcts.

2. She's so lively and smiley that her responses to the audience seem entirely unforced and _____ .

3. Most of them are trying to avoid _____ (head-on) confrontation with the organization.

4. There is a subtle message to the reader who sits _____ (ponder) the meaning of the titles.

5. The _____ (stigma) of having gone to prison will always be with me.

6. They readily understood how water _____ (erode) rock, and this made Lyell's report all the more believable.

7. There was much satisfaction in these stories: at last, the Newfoundlanders had found a vessel for the _____ (jibe) that had taunted them for years.

8. In February, 1968 the air _____ (above) this space was crowded with comings and goings.

9. My father did so many _____ (charity) things in his lifetime, we would like to continue that work in his good name and build on it.

10. It's best to watch them from the openings rather than swimming in, because you could damage the _____ (fragility) coral roofs and frighten them off.

IV. Translate the following sentences into Chinese.

1. Yes, money is one of the main things couples fight about. But having so much of it that you can give billions away doesn't eliminate the questions that every couple

faces: Do we still want similar things in life? Can we still create that life together? Or would it be better if we forged ahead on our own?

2. When Jeff and MacKenzie Bezos announced their intention to split in 2019, divorce lawyer Nicole Sodoma highlighted this universal challenge in staying together long-term. "The people we marry are not the people we divorce," she said, "because people change."

3. For many couples, the pandemic has made it impossible to ignore those shifts. The big pause of the past year kept couples home together for longer hours, canceled work travel and created new roles and routines unexpectedly, Sodoma says, forcing couples who were ignoring problems in their marriages to suddenly face them head-on.

4. "You go through phases in your marriage and you go through phases as a person, and sometimes they don't jibe," Larson notes. "When you have kids, you're on a path together." Once they're grown, you have to figure out what your shared path will be, Larson adds, or decide this isn't what you want anymore.

5. "We have a lot of scripts when we're young for how life should look," Larson says, adding that "there's no script for midlife. You get to create it on your own. That's both liberating and scary."

V. Topics for discussion.
1. What are the main reasons for the divorce of couples?
2. Please describe your ideal marriage.

8 Education

1. What are the responsibilities of a teacher in a public school?
2. What is the impact of the COVID-19 on education?
3. How can the government protect the rights and interests of both students and teachers?
4. What is your outlook for education in the post-pandemic era?

Part II Intensive Reading

Text A

In Defense of Our Teachers

When it comes to the daunting question of reopening schools, America's educators deserve a plan, not a trap.

I hate to break it to you, but I was a terrible student.

Each day, I desperately waited for the final bell to ring so that I could be released from the confines of my stuffy, windowless classroom and run home to my guitar. It was no fault of the Fairfax County Public Schools system, mind you; it did the best it could. I was just stubbornly disengaged, impeded by a raging case of ADD and an insatiable desire to play music. Far from being a model student, I tried my best to maintain focus, but eventually left school halfway through 11th grade to follow my dreams of becoming a professional touring musician. I left behind countless missed opportunities. To this day, I'm haunted by a recurring dream that I'm back in those crowded hallways, now struggling to graduate as a 51-year-old man, and anxiously wake in a pool of my own sweat. You can take the boy out of school, but you can't take school out of the boy! So, with me being a high-school dropout, you would imagine that the current debate surrounding the reopening of schools wouldn't register so much as a blip on my rock-and-roll radar, right? Wrong.

My mother was a public-school teacher.

As a single mother of two, she tirelessly devoted her life to the service of others, both at home and at work. From rising before dawn to ensure that my sister and I were bathed, dressed, and fed in time to catch the bus to grading papers well into the night, long after her dinner had gone cold, she rarely had a moment to herself. All this while working multiple jobs to supplement her meager $35,000 annual salary. Bloomingdale's, Servpro, SAT prep, GED prep — she even once coached soccer for a $400 stipend, funding our first family trip to New York City, where we stayed at the St. Regis Hotel and ordered drinks at its famous King Cole Bar so that we could fill up on the free hors d'oeuvres we otherwise could not afford. Unsurprisingly, her devoted parenting mirrored her technique as a teacher. Never one to just point at a blackboard and recite lessons for kids to mindlessly memorize, she was an engaging educator, invested in the well-being of each and every student who sat in her class. And at an average of 32 students a class, that was no small feat. She was one of those teachers who became a mentor to many, and her students remembered her long after they had graduated, often bumping into her at the grocery store and erupting into a full recitation of Shakespeare's *Julius Caesar*, like a flash mob in the produce aisle. I can't tell you how many of her former students I've met over the years who offer anecdotes from my mother's classroom. Every kid should be so lucky to have that favorite teacher, the one who changes your life for the better. She helped generations of children learn how to learn, and, like most other teachers, exhibited a selfless concern for others. Though I was never her student, she will forever be my favorite teacher.

It takes a certain kind of person to devote their life to this difficult and often-thankless job. I know because I was raised in a community of them. I have mowed their lawns, painted their apartments, even babysat their children, and I'm convinced that they are as essential as any other essential workers. Some even raise rock stars! Tom Morello of Rage Against the Machine, Adam Levine, Josh Groban, and Haim are all children of school workers (with hopefully more academically rewarding results than mine). Over the years, I have come to notice that teachers share a special bond, because there aren't too many people who truly understand their unique challenges — challenges that go far beyond just pen and paper. Today, those challenges could mean life or death for some.

When it comes to the daunting — and ever more politicized — question of reopening schools amid the coronavirus pandemic, the worry for our children's well-being is paramount. Yet teachers are also confronted with a whole new set of dilemmas that most people would not consider. "There's so much more to be addressed than just opening the doors and sending them back home," my mother tells me over the phone. Now 82 and retired, she runs down a list of concerns based on her 35 years of experience:"masks and distancing, temperature checks, crowded busing, crowded hallways, sports, air-conditioning systems, lunchrooms, public restrooms, janitorial staff." Most schools already struggle from a lack of resources; how could they possibly afford the mountain of safety measures that will need to be in place? And although the average age of a schoolteacher in the United States is in the early 40s, putting them in a lower-risk group, many career teachers, administrators, cafeteria workers, nurses, and janitors are older and at higher risk. Every school's working faculty is a considerable percentage of its population, and should be safeguarded appropriately. I can only imagine if my mother were now forced to return to a stuffy, windowless classroom. What would we learn from that lesson? When I ask what she would do, my mother replies, "Remote learning for the time being."

Remote learning comes with more than a few of its own complications, especially for working-class and single parents who are dealing with the logistical problem of balancing jobs with children at home. Uneven availability of teaching materials and online access, technical snafus, and a lack of socialization all make for a less-than-ideal learning experience. But most important, remote setups overseen by caretakers, with a teacher on the other end doing their best to educate distracted kids who prefer screens used for games, not math, make it perfectly clear that not everyone with a laptop and a dry-erase board is cut out to be a teacher. That specialized skill is the X factor. I know this because I have three children of my own, and my remote classroom was more *Welcome Back, Kotter* than *Dead Poets Society*. Like I tell my children, "You don't really want daddy helping, unless you want to get an F!" Remote learning is an inconvenient and hopefully temporary solution.

Every teacher has a "plan". Don't they deserve one too? My mother had to come up with three separate lesson plans every single day (public speaking, AP English, and English 10), because that's what teachers do: They provide you with the necessary tools to survive. Who is providing them with a set of their own? America's teachers are caught in a trap, set by indecisive and conflicting sectors of failed leadership that have never been in their position and can't possibly relate to the unique challenges they face. I wouldn't trust the US secretary of percussion to tell me how to play "Smells Like Teen Spirit" if they had never sat behind a drum set, so why should any teacher trust Secretary of Education Betsy DeVos to tell them how to teach, without her ever having sat at the head of a class? Until you have spent countless days in a classroom devoting your time and energy to becoming that lifelong mentor to generations of otherwise disengaged students, you must listen to those who have. Teachers want to teach, not die, and we should support and protect them like the national treasures that they are. For without them, where would we be?

May we show these tireless altruists a little altruism in return. I would for my favorite teacher. Wouldn't you?

Total words: 1,357

Total Reading Time: _____ minutes _____ seconds

Vocabulary

confine *n.* 限定；限制

stuffy *adj.* 闷热的；通风不畅的；古板的

impede *v.* 阻止；阻碍

insatiable *adj.* 不知足的；无法满足的

blip *n.* 目标（显示）标志；变故

meager *adj.* 少量且劣质的

stipend *n.* 薪俸；生活津贴

feat *n.* 功绩，武艺；技艺

mow *v.* 割；修剪

daunting *adj.* 使人胆怯的；使人气馁的

paramount *adj.* 至为重要的；首要的

janitorial *n.* 门卫；门警，管理员

snafu *n.* （一切均未按计划发生的）混乱局面

percussion *n.* 打击乐器

Phrases

fill up on 用……填满

hors d'oeuvres 开胃菜；冷盘，点心

for the time being 暂时；目前；眼下

Notes

ADD: ADD (attention deficit disorder) is the term commonly used to describe a neurological condition with symptoms of inattention, distractibility, and poor working memory. ADD symptoms in adults include trouble focusing on school work, habitually forgetting appointments, easily losing track of time, and struggling with executive functions. Patients with these symptoms may have what clinicians now call Predominantly Inattentive Type attention deficit hyperactivity disorder (ADHD). ADD is an outdated term and no longer a medical diagnosis, though it is often still used to refer to a certain subset of symptoms that fall under the umbrella term, ADHD.

Julius Caesar: The *Tragedy of Julius Caesar* is a history play and tragedy by William Shakespeare first performed in 1599.

flash mob: A flash mob (or flashmob) is a group of people who assemble suddenly in a public place, perform for a brief time, then quickly disperse, often for the purposes of entertainment, satire, and artistic expression. Flash mobs may be organized via telecommunications, social media, or viral emails.

Welcome Back, Kotter: *Welcome Back, Kotter* is an American sitcom starring Gabe Kaplan as a high school teacher in charge of a racially and ethnically diverse remedial class called the "Sweathogs". Recorded in front of a live studio audience, it originally aired on ABC from September 9, 1975, to May 17, 1979.

Dead Poets Society: *Dead Poets Society* is a 1989 American teen drama film written by Tom Schulman, directed by Peter Weir, and starring Robin Williams. Set in 1959 at the fictional elite conservative Vermont boarding school Welton Academy, it tells the story of an English teacher who inspires his students through his teaching of poetry.

Exercises

I. **Answer the following questions after reading the text.**

1. Why does the author say "you can take the boy out of school, but you can't take school out of the boy"?
2. What kind of teacher is the author's mother according her students?
3. What is the author's mother's concern about reopening schools amid the coronavirus pandemic?
4. What is the author's attitude towards his mother?
5. What is the author's purpose of writing this article?

II. **Decide whether the following statements are true or false according to the text.**

1. The author suffered from ADD at a very young age.
2. The author tried his best to maintain focus, but eventually left school halfway through 11th grade for his dreams of becoming a professional touring musician.
3. According to the author, remote learning is an inconvenient but temporary solution.
4. People in America including the author are firmly for the government's response towards the pandemic.
5. The condition of public school teachers in USA right now is particularly alarming.

III. **Fill in the blank of the following sentences with one of the words or phrases given below. Change the form where necessary.**

confine	stuffy	insatiable	meager	daunt
paramount	stipend	feat	mow	snafu

1. It needs to be planted away from buildings and underground pipes because it develops rather fat roots which are known to lift paving and crack pools if it is

_____ to too small a space.

2. He had laid off some heavy bets recently and his _____ earnings as a postman would not cover them.

3. Their parents can rest assured that their children's safety will be of _____ importance.

4. The junior doctors are demanding better amenities in all three medical colleges and the dental college, implementation of the senior residency scheme and regular payment of _____ .

5. This is different from those _____ rooms in other restaurants, compartments here have a big round window in each wall and large straw curtains.

6. These would be _____ never previously achieved and one could be excused for thinking of them as over-ambitious.

7. It has been a busy and successful year for the explorer and it seems his _____ appetite for doing the impossible is never-ending.

8. It was a hot day and the windows were open and the smell of newly _____ grass wafted in from the playing fields.

9. In recent years the defense and aerospace giant has weathered operational _____ , ethical scandals, criminal convictions, and abrupt executive departures.

10. Travelling alone around the world is a _____ prospect.

IV. Translate the following sentences into Chinese.

1. Each day, I desperately waited for the final bell to ring so that I could be released from the confines of my stuffy, windowless classroom and run home to my guitar. It was no fault of the Fairfax County Public Schools system, mind you; it did the best it could. I was just stubbornly disengaged, impeded by a raging case of ADD and an insatiable desire to play music.

2. And at an average of 32 students a class, that was no small feat. She was one of those teachers who became a mentor to many, and her students remembered her long after they had graduated, often bumping into her at the grocery store and erupting into a full recitation of Shakespeare's *Julius Caesar*, like a flash mob in the produce aisle.

3. Over the years, I have come to notice that teachers share a special bond, because there aren't too many people who truly understand their unique challenges — challenges that go far beyond just pen and paper. Today, those challenges could mean

life or death for some.

4. But most important, remote setups overseen by caretakers, with a teacher on the other end doing their best to educate distracted kids who prefer screens used for games, not math, make it perfectly clear that not everyone with alaptop and a dry-erase board is cut out tobe a teacher.

5. America's teachers are caught in a trap, set by indecisive and conflicting sectors of failed leadership that have never been in their position and can't possibly relate to the unique challenges they face.

V. Select one word for each blank from the following word bank. You may not use any of the words in the bank more than once. Change the form where necessary.

urged	online	infections	vaccination	minimize
prompt	despite	regard	warning	up-to-date

The number of COVID cases has risen sharply at some universities as about a million students begin to head home for the Christmas break, __1__ fears that the mass migration could fuel the spread of the virus.

Students have been urged to take COVID tests before they leave their university to travel to see their families — the vast majority on public transport — and again before they return in the new year, as well as getting their booster vaccinations.

But with case numbers increasing rapidly on some campuses, including Omicron infections, there are reports that students have decided to leave early to limit the risk of having to isolate over Christmas away from home.

Loughborough University and Imperial College London have moved learning __2__ for most students for the last few days of term after a significant uptick in cases. Elsewhere, universities have __3__ staff and students to either cancel or scale back planned Christmas celebrations to limit mixing.

About 30 universities finished at the end of last week, but for most term will end on Friday and universities are following government guidance to retain face-to-face teaching to the very end, ___4___ the prime minister's wider call for people to work from home in light of the rapid spread of Omicron.

Rowland Kao, a professor of epidemiology at the University of Edinburgh who contributes to the Spi-M modelling subgroup of the Scientific Advisory Group for Emergencies (SAGE), said outbreaks at universities had not been as severe as last year.

"However, any travel carries some risk and in particular has the potential for greater exposure during travel and also, importantly, to introduce mixing between age groups that would not be there at other times of the year.

"Thus students travelling should be cautious in ___5___ to both physical distancing measures and with the use of lateral flow tests to try to detect presymptomatic infections."

The University of Oxford reported a significant increase in ___6___, with more than 100 positive COVID-19 cases in the week ending 10 December and a 14% positivity rate, while the University of Sheffield reported a sharp rise to 81 cases among students on 14 December in a seven-day rolling average of 27.

Despite the increasing numbers there are no plans for staggered departures in December and for the January return, as were implemented last year to try to reduce the number of students travelling on the same day.

The government is instead relying on testing and high levels of ___7___ among students. According to the Office for National Statistics, 90% of higher education students have had at least one vaccine dose, and 78% have had two. Everyone aged over 18 is expected to be offered a booster vaccine by the end of December.

The University and College Union (UCU), which represents university staff, urged the government to allow universities to move online for the final week of term, rather than risk unnecessary infections and isolation over Christmas.

"Sadly, as was the case last year, the government and the vast majority of institutions have ignored ___8___ from staff and unions and taken unnecessary risks," said the UCU general secretary, Jo Grady. "With such poor leadership, it is little wonder some students have already voted with their feet and returned home for the year.

"The challenge now is delivering a safe return to learning in January. Universities must carry out new risk assessments before the start of the next academic term and ensure appropriate mitigations are in place to keep students and staff safe."

A Department for Education spokesperson called on students to get their booster jab and keep testing regularly. "To ___9___ the spread of Covid over the holidays we are urging every student heading home to get tested before they leave and to test before they go back in the new term, and we are working closely with the higher education sector to make sure students can continue to benefit from in-person teaching."

Universities UK, which represents 140 universities in England, Wales, Scotland and Northern Ireland, added: "Universities are working closely with the health authorities and relevant government departments and will follow the most ___10___ public health advice to help keep the university community safe."

Part III　Extensive Reading

Text B

Choosing Between Housing on or off Campus

The sticker price for off-campus housing may look cheaper, but students should be aware of hidden costs.

First-year college students often are expected or required to live in residence halls or dormitories. In subsequent years, it's usually up to those students to decide whether to reside on or off campus.

But some schools, like Ohio Wesleyan University and Dickinson College in Pennsylvania, don't provide an option. Both of these liberal arts colleges require four years of on-campus living. "We believe that living on campus for your entire time here during your college career really helps to complement your educational career," says George Stroud, vice president and dean of student life at Dickinson. "It connects you more with the campus, with the facilities, with your peers and with the faculty. It allows students to easily access programs and labs and things of that nature. And so we really believe that having students here on campus for the four years really helps to build a better community."

There are exceptions, however. At OWU, a student is exempt from the requirement if he or she is a commuter, fifth-year senior, at least 23 years of age, married, a parent to a dependent child, has medical or psychological needs that cannot be met by the institution or lives with parents or a legal guardian.

Living on campus has been shown to increase graduation and retention rates as well as improve academic performance, especially among first-year students, says Dwayne K. Todd, vice president of student engagement and success and dean of students at OWU.

"A number of indicators around success are quite clear in decades of research," he adds, "so that's why schools like ours do have a living requirement to create the best environment for student success."

Residential housing is not limited to shared dorm rooms and communal bathrooms. Other alternatives include suites, apartments, Greek houses or living-learning communities for students with shared interests.

On-campus students have access to services and resources such as residence life staff who can provide assistance if a housing issue arises.

"The social experience of living with so many fellow new students is a unique opportunity to make lifelong friendships," Brendon Dybdahl, spokesperson for university housing at the University of Wisconsin-Madison, wrote in an email. "Our staff can help students navigate roommate issues or move to another room if necessary, while students who live off-campus are locked into a lease with few options to manage roommate conflicts. We also have academic resources in our residence halls for tutoring, advising and class sections."

It can also be a safer environment, especially during the coronavirus pandemic as residential students were regularly monitored, quarantined and tested, says Rose Pascarell, vice president for university life at George Mason University in Virginia.

"We have a vaccine clinic on campus," she adds. "There's also a health clinic on campus staffed by physicians, nurse practitioners and physician assistants that residential students have access to ... I can tell you on any given week how many students on campus had tested positive. We had a way to quarantine those students in a residence hall that was off limits to everyone except those that were exposed."

On the other hand, off-campus living provides a student with more independence, as he or she is not constrained to school housing policies. It can also be better for students with severe food allergies or dietary restrictions, according to Cyndy McDonald, a career coach in California and member of the Independent Educational Consultants Association.

Cost Comparison

At first glance, off-campus housing can appear as the less-expensive option. But the additional expenses outside of rent like utilities, groceries, Internet access, cable and furniture are often overlooked.

"I would encourage students to really read their contracts," says Lisa Ortiz, interim director of housing and residence life at Ferris State University in Michigan. "That is something that I've heard from students that they don't realize those hidden fees and the different aspects of what the contracts are truly telling them in terms of cleaning and other things as they move out of the apartment. So we definitely want our students to fully understand what they're committing to."

To reduce off-campus costs, some students choose to overpack houses or apartments, sometimes with four or five people in a two-bedroom house, experts say.

But unlike off-campus housing, the total cost of living on campus is typically all-inclusive — covering rent, utilities, furniture, Wi-Fi and a meal plan.

At GMU, where students are encouraged to live on campus for at least the first year, the average cost of a traditional double room with an "Independence Plan" — the mandatory meal plan for residential freshman and sophomores with unlimited access to dining halls — is $12,630 for the 2021–2022 school year. The school estimates off-campus housing — outside of living with parents — to be $13,268, but prices can be higher or lower based on number of residents.

Another factor that plays into cost is the length of a lease. Residence halls follow an academic schedule while landlords at off-campus properties often require a full year. In such cases, students not taking summer classes must either pay for an additional three months or, if permitted, sublet to a replacement tenant.

Some experts say it's a toss-up between the price differences of living on or off campus because costs can vary based on many components, including location and convenience. Therefore, when making a decision about housing, students should consider more than just the price tag.

"Take a look at your grades, see how you're doing," says Russell Mast, vice president for student affairs at Morehead State University in Kentucky. "If you're struggling then I would say try to stay on campus because those support units are there for you. But if you know how to balance life, if you're good at time management and budgeting, then take a look at living off campus."

Financial Aid Options

Though prices are comparable, schools like Ferris State offer financial incentives to students who choose to live on campus. Admitted students can earn up to $2,000, for example, through the school's Bulldog Housing Bonus program. To qualify, a student must attend a virtual housing information session and submit a housing contract.

Financial aid is also available for off-campus living.

When filling the Free Application for Federal Student Aid, also known as the FAFSA, a student indicates whether he or she plans to live on campus, off campus or with a parent. A set budget is allocated to each student by a college that can be used for rent, utilities, groceries and other housing-related expenses. If the aid does not cover the full cost of rent for the year, students can file an appeal, and documentation is required, according to McDonald.

She adds that student loans are most commonly used to help pay room and board fees.

"Don't hesitate to ask the financial aid office," McDonald says. "There's nothing wrong with being the squeaky wheel. If you don't know, keep asking. And there's nothing wrong with writing an appeal. If you are not getting enough money and you need a little bit more then don't be afraid to ask for more. All they can do is say no. But they can't say yes if you don't ask."

Total words: 1,280

Total Reading Time: _____ minutes_____ seconds

💬 Vocabulary

utility *n.* 公用事业；水电费
interim *adj.* 暂时的；过渡的；中间的；间歇的
overpack *v.* 过度包装；过多挤进；过多塞入
mandatory *adj.* 法定的；强制的；义务的
sublet *v.* 转租
toss-up *n.*（两种选择、结果等的）同样可能；均等机会
incentive *n.* 激励刺激；鼓励

Phrases

have access to 接近；得到
be constrained to 被······限制，被······约束

Exercises

I. Answer the following questions after reading the text.

1. What is George Stroud's attitude towards living on campus?
2. According to the cost comparison, which one is cheaper? On-campus or off-campus?
3. What are the factors that play importantly into the cost?
4. In order to be qualified in the Bulldog Housing Bonus program, what action should students take?
5. Which way of living would you choose when you're in university?

II. Decide whether the following statements are true or false according to the text.

1. According to the essay, living on campus for the entire time there during one's college career really helps to complement the educational career because it connects students more with the campus, with the facilities, with peers and with the faculty.
2. Brendon says that living on campus has been shown to increase graduation and retention rates as well as improve academic performance, especially among first-year students.
3. Living off campus also has its advantages for it provides a student with more independence.
4. Financial aid is not available for off-campus living.
5. If you have any question on living on-campus, do not hesitate to ask help from the financial aid office.

III. Fill in the blanks with the words given in the brackets. Change the form where necessary.

1. I'm sure there's some _____ (utility) in emergency services practicing working together, but this seems far too choreographed to root out real bugs in the response system.
2. Whoever they get I suggest that they should get someone as soon as possible in order to ensure that players don't leave in the _____ (interim).
3. The show wasn't high content even though the gallery was way _____ (overpack).
4. The unanimous decision means the 61-year-old faces a _____ (mandatory) life sentence.
5. The respondent's lease contained a covenant against _____ (sublet); and the

superior landlord might well wish to be heard on the question whether or not there was an existing sub-tenancy.

6. He may be Sweden's most talented player, but it's a _____ (toss-up) as to whether he'll be making the headlines for his on- or off-the-field behaviour.

7. If bad deeds are encouraged and condoned, this merely provides an _____ (incentive) for them to multiply.

8. It is difficult to get food to Seliyarovo because the 420-person village is only _____ (access) by car or helicopter.

9. I am not _____ (constrain) to continue working on this piece if I need some alternative activity.

10. I hope this article will offer insight into the risks, benefits, and indications for use of this _____ (diet) therapy.

IV. Translate the following sentences into Chinese.

1. "A number of indicators around success are quite clear in decades of research," he adds, "so that's why schools like ours do have a living requirement to create the best environment for student success."

2. On the other hand, off-campus living provides a student with more independence, as he or she is not constrained to school housing policies. It can also be better for students with severe food allergies or dietary restrictions, according to Cyndy McDonald, a career coach in California and member of the Independent Educational Consultants Association.

3. At first glance, off-campus housing can appear as the less-expensive option. But the additional expenses outside of rent like utilities, groceries, Internet access, cable and furniture are often overlooked.

4. Another factor that plays into cost is the length of a lease. Residence halls follow an academic schedule while landlords at off-campus properties often require a full year. In such cases, students not taking summer classes must either pay for an additional three months or, if permitted, sublet to a replacement tenant.

5. "Don't hesitate to ask the financial aid office," McDonald says. "There's nothing wrong with being the squeaky wheel. If you don't know, keep asking. And there's nothing wrong with writing an appeal. If you are not getting enough money and you need a little bit more then don't be afraid to ask for more. All they can do is say no. But they can't say yes if you don't ask."

V. Topics for discussion.
  1. What characteristics should a qualified educator have?
  2. Please describe an unforgettable lesson that you have ever had.

Unit 9 Career

Part I   Pre-reading Questions

1. How do you understand the sentence "a career is a marathon not a sprint"?
2. What would you do to make yourself shine on a CV?
3. Do you think it is necessary to take risks in you career in order to grow and stretch yourself?
4. What is the skillset that you should build in your career journey?

Part II   Intensive Reading

Text A

The Big Decisions that Impact Your Career

One of the best things about being a young professional is the limitless number of possibilities that lie ahead of you. Especially for those in the earliest stages of your career, there are so many options available — so many industries and interests you can potentially tap into.

But, at the same time, this can feel pretty overwhelming. How do you know which direction is the right one to take?

While some people argue that your first job doesn't really matter, I've found it surprising just how often the choices people make in their early 20s impact their job paths in the longer term. That's why, before you make any big decisions, it's worth taking a step back and being strategic.

A career is a marathon not a sprint — and yours will benefit from a good strategy. I recommend you start by making these four choices that I've seen prove successful for my clients throughout their professional journeys.

Work at companies that specialize in your skillset

There is plenty of good advice out there around how to make yourself shine on a CV, no matter your role. But it is because of this plethora of advice that it can be difficult for hiring managers to distinguish if you will be successful once hired, or if you're just good at presenting yourself on paper.

Having a couple of recognizable brand names on your résumé — specifically brands that have a strong reputation in your sector or area of specialization — can help you stand out from the crowd. This is especially true later on in your career when you are more likely to be competing for executive or leadership positions.

What do I mean exactly by "brands"? These are companies that people in your industry have heard about and respect. I'm not necessarily referring to big and elusive organizations like Apple, Amazon, or Google (where the acceptance rate is a mere 0.2%). My advice is a bit broader and more realistic: Look into organizations that people in your profession, or in your future dream job, will probably recognize and have positive associations with.

For instance, if you work in IT industry, you are better off having a niche (but innovative) technology company on your résumé than a well-known consumer goods business. Likewise, if you work in marketing, it looks better to have experience at a consumer-facing company than to have spent five years at a huge tech start-up.

In my experience, when you focus on roles in an industry that value your particular kind of work, recruiters and hiring managers will assume — rightly or not — that you have learned from the best, or from people at an organization where your skills are highly valued and important to the business.

Choose to work with people whom you want in your network

As I'm sure you've heard before, the majority of roles are found through networking. In fact, a recent study found that this is the case 85% of the time. Networking comes from building relationships: working with people, being helpful to people in your network, and staying in touch. Before choosing any new role (whether it is your first, second, or third), it is a good idea to look at who you will be on your team, as these people could become important contacts and references down the line.

Work with the best people that you can: people who have impressive experiences, people with a track record of success and promotion, and people with whom you have good chemistry and you can see yourself keeping in touch long-term. This applies to your seniors, but also to your teammates. Connect with peers who are as ambitious as you are and will think of you when future opportunities arise.

How do you find these people?

Sometimes it will be intuitive. There will always be certain co-workers with whom you immediately connect because of shared values or goals, and these relationships usually have the potential to last longer term. When it comes to your seniors, look for leaders who have a track record of giving people in their networks good opportunities. Oftentimes, this may be a manager who has brought a former employee onto their team after changing roles or companies. The fact that they have stayed connected suggests that they value loyalty and are willing to support people on their career journeys.

Look for opportunities to grow and stretch yourself

If you're an ambitious employee, you may be eager to get promoted as quickly as possible. But there are times when it is more useful to make a strategic lateral move that is related to your current role and a bit outside of your comfort zone. The first decade of your career is a great time to take risks, build transferable skills, and develop some technical expertise.

For instance, if you work in marketing and you have an opportunity to make a move into sales, think of it as a way for you to acquire skills in an adjacent field. Likewise, if you work in consumer goods, where brand and product development are critical, consider spending some time in a marketing position to get a better perspective on how marketing activities turn products into revenue.

Stretching yourself may seem scary at first, but remember that we all need to experience challenges, and even failures, before we can build resilience, learn, and develop new and better skills. It's best to do this earlier in your career, when mistakes are less visible, and when there is plenty of time to learn from your mistakes and come out better for it.

If you use your first few jobs to gain a deep understanding of the roles and departments that exist within your sector — and how they work together to meet their collective goals — you will be a more competitive candidate for leadership roles down the line.

Once you move into a senior role, you will likely have less "hands on" responsibilities and oversee more of the employees who do. This is when that foundational knowledge you've been building will come into play. You'll need to know how different teams function, as well as what they need from you as a leader to do their jobs well.

Don't get distracted by shortcuts

There are so many ideas about how you can "short cut" the hard work of gaining good experience and building your network over time. Some people suggest focusing on your "personal brand" by making cosmetic improvements to your CV and growing your social media channels. Others suggest taking the start-up route for a fast track to the top.

There are caveats with both of these suggestions to keep in mind.

First, when it comes to personal branding, remember that people can see through hot air. The truth is that there will never be a substitute for doing great work and building out strong experiences. When you are promoting yourself there needs to be real substance behind it — and if there is, hiring managers will see that.

Second, when it comes to start-ups, remember that there are definitely great companies out there but pursuing a start-up role is a high-risk, high-reward decision. Even if you are lucky enough to join the next Amazon, there will be long hours, worries about failure, and lots of pressure. Before accepting a role in this world, be sure to ask lots of questions about the business and their future plans. Check out the experience of the management team to see if you are confident in their leadership skills. If you see or hear something you don't like, then think twice.

When it comes to larger roles that come later in careers, employers are discerning and selective. This is when they rely on the power of corporate brands and references from well-known people to separate out candidates with verifiable experience.

The strongest way to secure these high-profile roles down the line is to put in the work right now: Grow your skills, take on lateral responsibilities, and work at companies and with people who will build up your credibility.

Total words: 1,355

Total Reading Time: _____ minutes _____ seconds

Vocabulary

skillset *n.* 技能组合

plethora *n.* 过多；过量；过剩

elusive *adj.* 难找的；难以解释的；难以达到的

chemistry *n.* 化学；化学成分；（常指有强烈性吸引力的）两人间的关系

intuitive *adj.* 直觉的；有直觉力的；易懂的，使用简便的

lateral *adj.* 侧面的，横向的

　　　　n. 侧部；[语]边音

revenue *n.* 财政收入；税收；收入，收益

collective *adj.* 集体的，共同的；共有的

　　　　　n. 合作农场，集体企业；企业集团

cosmetic *adj.* 装门面的，表面的；整容的

　　　　　n. 化妆品，美容品

caveat *n.* 警告；告诫

substitute *n.* 替代品，代替物；替补（运动员）

　　　　　v. 代替；取代

discerning *adj.* 有识别力的；有洞察力的

verifiable *adj.* 可证实的；能作证的；可检验的

credibility *n.* 可靠性，可信性

Phrases

tap into 开发；探寻；利用

better off 境况较好的

come into play 开始活动；开始起作用

Notes

CV: CV is the abbreviation for curriculum vitae (a written record of your education and the jobs you have done, which you send when you are applying for a job).

Amazon: Amazon is a massive online retailer that has a market capitalization as of June 2018 that is in excess of $268 billion. As well as being an online retailer, Amazon allows for individuals and businesses to sell and display products for sale on line. It is the largest Internet retailer in the world by revenue, with 2017 revenues of more than $177 billion.

niche technology: A niche technology is a technological system that is used by a segmented audience based on location, interests, demographics, and price.

comfort zone: The comfort zone is a safe space where we don't risk, but neither do we grow. It's not simply a physical space but a mental concept. It's not limited to a secure cord we've built around us but includes both our daily routines and way of thinking.

Exercises

I. **Answer the following questions after reading the text.**

1. What are the four choices the author recommend to start your career?

2. According to the text, why are "brand names" important on your résumé?

3. How do you build relationships for your networking?

4. What does "stretching yourself" refer to for young employee?

5. What is the strongest way to secure these high-profile roles down the line?

II. **Decide whether the following statements are true or false according to the text.**

1. One of the best things about being a young professional is the limited number of possibilities that lie ahead of you.

2. Before you make any big decisions, it's worth taking a step back and being strategic.

3. A career is a marathon not a sprint — and yours will benefit from a good strategy.

4. If you work in marketing, it looks better to have spent five years at a huge tech start-up than to have experience at a consumer-facing company.

5. If you're an ambitious employee, you may be eager to get promoted as quickly as possible.

III. **Fill in the blank of the following sentences with one of the words or phrases given below. Change the form where necessary.**

collective	intuitive	lateral	credibility	resilience
cosmetic	verifiable	substitute	elusive	adjacent

1. This kind of stability is also called _____ .
2. The schools were _____ but there were separate doors.
3. Mr. Dawson walked into the court from a _____ door.
4. Her _____ was telling her that something was wrong.
5. Both of us are biologists, so we swerved to talk about the_____ chameleon.
6. Though its villain also receives his rightful deserts, the thriller presents a less comfortable and _____ world.
7. This is not a romantic notion but _____ fact.
8. She is seeking a _____ for the very man whose departure made her cry.
9. She received a _____ makeover at a beauty salon as a birthday gift.
10. The cabinet is _____ responsible for policy.

IV. Translate the following sentences into Chinese.

1. While some people argue that your first job doesn't really matter, I've found it surprising just how often the choices people make in their early 20s impact their job paths in the longer term.

2. But it is because of this plethora of advice that it can be difficult for hiring managers to distinguish if you will be successful once hired, or if you're just good at presenting yourself on paper.

3. Work with the best people that you can: people who have impressive experiences, people with a track record of success and promotion, and people with whom you have good chemistry and you can see yourself keeping in touch long-term.

4. The first decade of your career is a great time to take risks, build transferable skills, and develop some technical expertise.

5. For instance, if you work in marketing and you have an opportunity to make a move into sales, think of it as a way for you to acquire skills in an adjacent field.

V. Select one word for each blank from the following word bank. You may not use any of the words in the bank more than once. Change the form where necessary.

| prime | defer | mentors | restless | consulting |
| discipline | profound | coined | identity | emerge |

Every four years, something inside me shifts. I get __1__ and want to learn something new or apply my skills in a new way. It's as though I shed a professional skin and start over, fresh.

In my 20s, I got all kinds of flak for this. When I decided to guide hiking trips rather than join a __2__ firm, my peers said that my résumé made no sense. When I opted to __3__ graduate school to travel in India, my __4__ questioned my seriousness and said my professional future could crash.

I felt like something was wrong with me because I was interested in so many things while my friends were laser-focused on climbing the corporate ladder. It's not that I wasn't __5__ or willing to work hard. There was just too much worth learning and doing. To settle on one pursuit seemed like a mistake.

Today, the world has changed in some amazing and __6__ ways. Broadening your career focus and professional __7__ is no longer seen as abnormal. It's celebrated. The macro forces driving the future of work demand independent and adaptable thinkers. When we add in the potential for automation to transform jobs *en masse*, the Great Resignation, and the growing number of hybrid offices around the world, it's clear that the time is ripe to rethink what a successful career path looks like.

Up until this point, we have lacked the language necessary to design our careers in ways that veer from the traditional script. But now there is hope. A new vocabulary is __8__. At the heart of it is a shift from pursuing a "career path" to creating your "career portfolio". This term was originally __9__ by philosopher and organizational behavior expert Charles Handy in the 1990s, and is poised to finally enter its __10__ today.

Part III **Intensive Reading**

Text B

Reshaping Your Career in the Wake of the Pandemic

Over the past year, we've all heard that we should be preparing for the "new normal" — but what that means or when this will start is unclear. During the pandemic, some professionals had to put their career aspirations on the back burner as they dealt with unexpected health care or childcare responsibilities, and many others may have felt their hard-fought career progression stall because of unpredictable outside forces, including company and industry disruptions.

It's clearly too soon to declare an end to the pandemic. But as vaccination takes hold and at least some countries and regions begin to open up, we remain hopeful about the potential changes on the horizon. Now is a useful time to begin asking yourself how to take back control over your career (Indeed, in our own research, we found that an opportunistic mindset is one of the foundational traits underlying entrepreneurial talent).

As we move into hybrid offices and hybrid professional identities, we're entering what social scientists call a "liminal" moment — the (sometimes uncomfortable) "in-between" phase when you're exiting a previous way of being and entering another. That creates uncertainty, but also opportunity. We've identified three key aspects of work that the pandemic has impacted and which — if you approach them thoughtfully and strategically — can help you reshape your career successfully for the future.

The manner in which we work

One thing we all learned this year, after being forced to adapt to specific ways of working, is how we best work. The pandemic has been an experiment like no other: a vehicle to understand what we need to thrive in our jobs, and what mode of working is best suited for our temperament.

Some professionals have thrived in a remote work environment and never want to go back. Others miss the social company of their colleagues and, gripped by loneliness, recognize that office life suits them well. The pandemic certainly validated the feasibility of virtual work — and once a privilege (as remote arrangements used to be seen) has been granted, they're very hard to take away. Meta-analytic studies have long shown that remote work is mostly beneficial — improving not just productivity and job satisfaction, but also family relations — or neutral. We can expect this to improve even more, thanks to both increased technological resources and a cultural readiness to accept that workplace results matter more than one's location.

That means, in many professions, it's likely you'll have far more freedom moving forward to shape, and maybe even control, the terms by which you'll work. In Dorie's forthcoming book *The Long Game*, she shares the story of Annmarie Neal, a successful HR executive who for more than 25 years — even pre-pandemic — managed to convince her employers to let her work from a small town in the Colorado mountains. She'd ask potential employers, "Do you want to hire the best person for the role, or the best person in your zip code?" Post-COVID, many more employees will be in a position to pose that same question.

The company and leaders we work for

Crises are often the truest test of leadership: under great pressure, good leaders excel, whereas bad leaders have nowhere to hide. During the pandemic, many people have learned new things about their boss and the senior leadership of their company. Did they treat their employees fairly and with respect? How did they navigate uncertainty? Did they prioritize the short-term or the long-term?

Armed with this new information, once employees feel the pandemic has stabilized, it's likely we'll see accelerated job turnover that may have been deferred for the past year. One study suggests that close to half of employees would quit if a hybrid option isn't granted, for instance. Given companies' increased openness to virtual arrangements, employees' options will also increase, because they're not limited by physical proximity. More than ever, you'll now have the opportunity to identify companies that share your values and potentially join forces with them, regardless of geography.

Our professional networks

The past year has also taught us whom we can rely on. Which coworkers stepped up to help you when you were facing personal challenges, or were staring down a major deadline? Which made the effort to stay connected, and which reverted to a purely transactional relationship, only getting in touch when they needed something from you? As we slowly return to in-person work and travel, our relationships are also likely to change, and we'll have a better sense of whom we want to bring closer in our lives, and whom we should deprioritize because they've proven themselves to be less caring or less reliable than we previously thought.

Additionally, after a year of isolation in which it's been much harder to meet new people, it's likely that many professionals are hungry to build new connections. If you make the effort to organize networking events — whether virtual or in-person (where safe and possible) — you'll likely reap disproportionate benefits by dint of being an "early mover" as people slowly begin to feel comfortable congregating again. This includes building a reputation as a "connector" and perhaps gaining access to interesting or prominent people that otherwise may have been hard to access because — quite simply — there is a dearth of other invitations for the time being. This is a liminal moment for relationships, as well, and provides a unique opportunity both to solidify deeper ties with trusted colleagues and to expand your overall network dramatically.

In short, there's a very real possibility that, thanks to the greater flexibility and opportunities enabled by the crisis, far more professionals may have the opportunity to craft work and careers they truly enjoy. As Antonio Gramsci, the great political theorist once noted, "a crisis consists precisely in the fact that the old is dying and the new cannot be born; in this interregnum a great variety of morbid symptoms appear." The past year has been challenging and discomfiting in so many ways — but we're optimistic that it might yet give birth to something new, and better.

Total words: 1,010

Total Reading Time: _____ minutes _____ seconds

Vocabulary

aspiration *n.* 渴望,抱负,志向;送气

disruption *n.* 扰乱,中断

vaccination *n.* 接种疫苗

entrepreneurial *adj.* 具有企业家素质的,富于企业家精神的

temperament *n.* 气质,性格;(性情)暴躁,喜怒无常

thrive *v.* 茁壮成长,兴旺发达,繁荣

feasibility *n.* 可行性,可能性

neutral *adj.* 中立的,中性的,不含褒贬义的;淡素的,素净的
　　　　n.(车辆排挡的)空挡;中立者,中立国;素净色,中和色

readiness *n.* 准备就绪;愿意

transactional *adj.* 交易的;事务性的;相互作用的

symptom *n.* 症状;征兆,征候

discomfit *v.* 使困惑;使窘迫;使尴尬

Phrases

hybrid office 混合办公室

remote work 远程办公

physical proximity 物理接近

Notes

Dorie Clark: Dorie Clark is the author of "Reinventing You: Define Your Brand, Imagine Your Future" (Harvard Business Review Press, 2013). A former presidential campaign spokeswoman, she is also a frequent contributor to the *Harvard Business Review* and *Forbes*. Recognized as a "branding expert" by the Associated Press and *Fortune*, Clark is a marketing strategy consultant and speaker for clients including Google, Microsoft, Yale University, Fidelity, and the World Bank.

Colorado: Colorado is classified as one of the mountain states, although only about half of its area lies in the Rocky Mountains. It borders Wyoming and Nebraska to the north, Nebraska and Kansas to the east, Oklahoma and New Mexico to the south, and Utah to the west.

Antonio Gramsci: Antonio Gramsci (January 23, 1891, Ales, Sardinia, Italy — April 27, 1937, Rome), is an intellectual and politician, a founder of the Italian Communist Party whose ideas greatly influenced Italian communism.

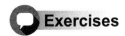 **Exercises**

I. Answer the following questions after reading the text.

1. What are the three key aspects of work that the pandemic has impacted identified in the passage?

2. What do we know about the "new normal"?

3. Is remote work mostly beneficial according to meta-analytic studies?

4. How do you understand the sentence "crises are often the truest test of leadership"?

5. How do the authors view the crisis brought by the pandemic?

II. Decide whether the following statements are true or false according to the text.

1. It's clearly time to declare an end to the pandemic.

2. One thing we all learned this year, after being forced to adapt to specific ways of working, is how we best work.

3. Crises are often the truest test of leadership: under great pressure, good leaders excel, whereas bad leaders have nowhere to hide.

4. Given companies' increased openness to virtual arrangements, employees' options will also increase, because they're limited by physical proximity.

5. Additionally, after a year of isolation in which it's been much harder to meet new people, it's likely that many professionals are hungry to build new connections.

III. Fill in the blanks with the words given in the brackets. Change the form where necessary.

1. My biggest _____ (aspire) in life is to be able to see the world and experience new and different ways of thinking.

2. A stroke can _____ (disruption) the supply of oxygen to the brain.

3. Now, children aged six months to five years are to be offered the _____ (vaccination) from next month.

4. He was eager to return to a more _____ (entrepreneur) role in which he had a big financial stake in his own efforts.

5. Her mental capacity and _____ (temperament) are as remarkable as his.

6. The place has rapidly developed from a small fishing community into a _____ (thrive) tourist resort.

7. The committee will study the _____ (feasible) of setting up a national computer network.

8. Security tightened in the capital in _____ (ready) for the president's arrival.

9. He said the crisis could _____ (acceleration) industry consolidation by forcing small producers out of business.

10. If you can take some of the pressure off of us, we might be able to _____ (solid) our position.

IV. Translate the following sentences into Chinese.

1. It's clearly too soon to declare an end to the pandemic. But as vaccination takes hold and at least some countries and regions begin to open up, we remain hopeful about the potential changes on the horizon.

2. As we move into hybrid offices and hybrid professional identities, we're entering what social scientists call a "liminal" moment — the (sometimes uncomfortable) "in-between" phase when you're exiting a previous way of being and entering another.

3. Some professionals have thrived in a remote work environment and never want to go back. Others miss the social company of their colleagues and, gripped by loneliness, recognize that office life suits them well.

4. Crises are often the truest test of leadership: under great pressure, good leaders excel, whereas bad leaders have nowhere to hide.

5. More than ever, you'll now have the opportunity to identify companies that share your values and potentially join forces with them, regardless of geography.

V. Topics for discussion.

1. How important is career planning for you?
2. What are the advantages and disadvantages the pandemic brings to your career?

Unit 10 Entertainment

Part I Pre-reading Questions

1. In what ways do you think entertainment can change our life?
2. What are the ways of entertainment in your favorite holiday?
3. How do you think of the deeds of the artists in protecting the environment?
4. What are the responsibilities for artists in modern society?

Part II Intensive Reading

Text A

The Art Exploring the Truth About How Climate Change Began

It has been more than three decades since climate change became front-page news. In 1988, *The New York Times* ran an article titled "Global Warming Has Begun, Expert Tells Senate". Ever since, discussions on the crisis have predominantly focused on how the state of the world has been affected by humans since the Industrial Revolution in the West — and with good reason. The Earth's temperature has increased by 0.07 ℃ every decade since the late 19th Century, a rise that has been linked to the mass burning of fossil fuels. Yet a new exhibition of work by various artists suggests that we must look further back in time and analyze the issue from a non-Western perspective in order to get a fuller picture of the current emergency.

The group show *We Are History: Race, Colonialism and Climate Change* opened to coincide with 1–54 Contemporary African Art Fair at London's Somerset House. Through the lens of 11 artists who have a personal relationship with the Caribbean, South America and Africa, the exhibition looks not only at the roots of global warming, but also at how it impacts the developing world. By looking back, the link between the world's environmental issues, colonialism and slavery is highlighted. Also explored is how these problems still have a disproportionately negative impact on certain countries. A study released in 2020, published by two archaeologists, revealed how colonization forced residents in Caribbean communities to move away from traditional and resilient ways of building homes to more modern but less suitable ways. These habitats have proved to be more difficult to maintain, with the materials needed for upkeep not locally available, and the buildings easily overwhelmed by hurricanes, putting people at greater risk during natural disasters.

Among the exhibits is Barbadian-Scottish artist Alberta Whittle's film *From the Forest to the Concrete (To the Forest)*, 2019, which directly explores this topic, documenting the effects of Hurricane Dorian in the Bahamas. The 10-minute-long film is stamped with the date 09.09.2019, nine days after the disaster. "Africa produces 4% of the world's greenhouse gases, the whole continent, but yet it is so at the front line," Whittle told culture magazine *The Skinny*. The artist wants people in the UK to see the disparity between their own comfort and the relative lack of comfort of their non-Western counterparts. She intertwines a number of performances with footage of destruction. "[There was] a terrible hurricane that moved through the Bahamas last week," she said at the time of its premiere. "But what I see in the weather in the news in the UK, is 'Oh isn't this wonderful, we are about to go through a period of sunshine'."

What this exhibition asks is: who we are really talking about when we question how our collective actions are having an effect on the environment? According to the curator of the exhibition, Ekow Eshun, if we don't allow the people in emerging countries to speak for themselves, we force them out of the conversation and into one that isn't consistent with the facts. "Otherwise we end up repeating the same narratives that we've repeated for a long time that somehow people in the developing world are supporting characters in the drama, rather than communities that are directly affected [by climate change]," Eshun tells BBC Culture.

Similarly, British filmmaker Louis Henderson focuses on how the West is primarily responsible for the disruptions to the natural world that humans have caused in his almost 30-minute long video *The Sea is History*, 2016. Henderson adapts the poem of the same name by Caribbean poet Derek Walcott. In his poem, Walcott discusses the effects of colonization on a community's culture, and claims that the history of these places is hidden in the sea. The footage in Henderson's piece features mesmerising shots of Lake Enriquillo, a lake in the Dominican Republic that often floods due to rises in sea temperature.

Much like Whittle and Henderson, the collaborative duo Jennifer Allora and Guillermo Calzadilla explore how outsiders have impacted the Caribbean, but they take a different approach. Their screen-printing method for the series *Contracts* uses layers of black ink to taint the beautiful scenery they depict. "What seem to be conventional pictures of a beautiful destination are disrupted by a layer of a single colour ink, shrouding the idyll partly or completely," say the duo. "We live and work in Puerto Rico, a Caribbean island that, since the colonial period, has been systematically exploited for its natural resources... As climate change makes weather events more severe, from droughts to hurricanes, the already vulnerable island is put in an even more heightened state of precariousness."

Contract (AOC L), 2014, shown at the exhibition, is a piece that is part of the larger series. In it, the pair catalogue sites in Vieques , Puerto Rico, where palm trees were used as markers by the US military to highlight where hazard waste was disposed. The areas are now managed by the US Department of the Interior, Fish and Wildlife Service as conservation zones, according to the artists."This paradoxical designation denies the underlying environmental and health risks of the dumps — so toxic that in 2005 they were placed on the US Environmental Protection Agency's Superfund National Priorities List," they say.

Colombian artist Carolina Caycedo says that the only way to truly move forward is to listen to the people who are explicitly affected by these changes to the ecosystem. "We urgently need to look at what communities that are actually on the frontlines are proposing on a grassroot level, since they are the people who are directly impacted by the climate crisis," she tells BBC Culture. Her research based on art project, *Be Dammed*, investigates the environmental and social consequences of dams throughout Latin America. "By [looking at] different case studies in the Americas, I've had a chance to collaborate with some of these communities to highlight alternatives to these large infrastructures," she says.

While none of these artists offer a hyper-specific call to action, collectively they show how climate change has affected the countries they belong to, or associate themselves with, and the importance of putting global issues into perspective. As Eshun puts it: "I think it's important that those voices and those perspectives are heard and not simply as victims but heard as people who have agency and autonomy, and in this respect they're heard through the voice of artists."

Total words: 1,063

Total Reading Time: _____ minutes _____ seconds

💬 **Vocabulary**

run *v.* 发表；刊登
predominantly *adv.* 主要地；多数情况下
perspective *n.* 态度，观点；透视法
resilient *adj.* 有适应力的，能复原的；有弹性的
habitat *n.* (动植物的) 生活环境，栖息地
upkeep *n.* 维修；维修费；保养
disparity *n.* 不等；不同；差异
intertwine *v.* 缠绕；紧密相连
emerging *adj.* 新兴的
　　　　v. 浮现，出现；显露，知悉
primarily *adv.* 主要地；根本地
adapt *v.* 适应；使适合；改编；改写
mesmerizing *adj.* 迷人的，有魅力的

💬 Phrases

coincide with 与……一致
look back 回顾
speak for 为……辩护；为……说话

💬 Notes

Industrial Revolution: Industrial Revolution is a rapid major change in an economy (as in England in the late 18th century) marked by the general introduction of power-driven machinery or by an important change in the prevailing types and methods of use of such machines.

Hurricane Dorian: Hurricane Dorian was the fourth named storm, second hurricane, and first major hurricane of the 2019 Atlantic hurricane season. Dorian formed on August 24, 2019 from a tropical wave in the Central Atlantic and gradually strengthened as it moved toward the Lesser Antilles, becoming a hurricane on August 28. Rapid intensification occurred, and on August 31, Dorian became a Category 4 hurricane.

Derek Walcott: Derek Walcott was born on January 23, 1930 in Castries, Saint Lucia. He was a writer and director, known for *Haytian Earth* (1984), *The Fist* (2017) and *NBC Experiment in Television* (1967). He was married to Sigrid Nama, Norline Metivier, Margaret Ruth Maillard and Fay Moston. He died on March 17, 2017 in Cap Estate, Gros-Islet, Saint Lucia.

Lake Enriquillo: Lake Enriquillo is a beautiful, hot, and magic spot in the southwest of the Dominican Republic. It is the largest and most hypersaline lake in the Caribbean. The water in the lake can reach hypersaline levels up to 66% higher than sea water.

💬 Exercises

I. **Answer the following questions after reading the text.**

1. How long has climate change become front-page new?
2. What is Alberta Whittle's film mainly about?
3. What did Alberta Whittle want people to do when she told culture magazine *The Skinny*?
4. How should the West be primarily responsible for the disruptions to the natural world according to Henderson's video?
5. Why does Carolina Caycedo say that the only way to truly move forward is to listen to the people who are explicitly affected by these changes to the ecosystem?

II. **Decide whether the following statements are true or false according to the text.**

1. It has been more than three decades since climate change became front-page news.
2. The Earth's temperature has increased by 0.07℃ every decade since the late 18th century,

a rise that has been linked to the mass burning of fossil fuels.

3. Among the exhibits is Barbadian-Scottish artist Alberta Whittle's book *From the Forest to the Concrete (To the Forest)*, 2019, which directly explores this topic, documenting the effects of Hurricane Dorian in the Bahamas.

4. In his poem, Walcott discusses the effects of colonization on a community's culture, and claims that the history of these places is hidden in the sea.

5. Much like Whittle and Henderson, the collaborative duo Jennifer Allora and Guillermo Calzadilla explore how outsiders have impacted the Caribbean, but they take a different approach.

III. **Fill in the blanks of the following sentences with one of the words or phrases given below. Change the form where necessary.**

primary	upkeep	speak for	look back	emerge
predominantly	resilient	run	habitat	intertwine

1. He made up his mind to enjoy his guitar and to accumulate as many happy experiences as he could so that when he retired he would be able to _____ on his life with satisfaction.

2. These people _____ themselves, uttering words they formulated themselves for the audience before them, and the audience isn't expected to interrupt.

3. The newspaper _____ a series of four editorials entitled "The Choice of Our Lives".

4. The plants in these colonies also need tough _____ stems above the soil, stems that can bent a lot but not break as water constantly crashes into them.

5. Evidence points to hunting by humans and _____ destruction as the likely causes for the current mass extinction.

6. The publication chronicles the building's design and construction history and proposes policies for its _____.

7. Their political careers had become closely _____.

8. The color you choose will be determined by the _____ color of the room.

9. But researchers say there are many other factors working against another Einstein _____ anytime soon.

10. During those years, several things happened, _____ linguistic or thematic and both involving secularization.

IV. **Translate the following sentences into Chinese.**

1. In 1988, *The New York Times* ran an article titled "Global Warming Has Begun,

Expert Tells Senate". Ever since, discussions on the crisis have predominantly focused on how the state of the world has been affected by humans since the Industrial Revolution in the West — and with good reason.

2. These habitats have proved to be more difficult to maintain, with the materials needed for upkeep not locally available, and the buildings easily overwhelmed by hurricanes, putting people at greater risk during natural disasters.

3. Among the exhibits is Barbadian-Scottish artist Alberta Whittle's film *From the Forest to the Concrete (To the Forest)*, 2019, which directly explores this topic, documenting the effects of Hurricane Dorian in the Bahamas.

4. Similarly, British filmmaker Louis Henderson focuses on how the West is primarily responsible for the disruptions to the natural world that humans have caused in his almost 30-minute long video *The Sea is History*, 2016.

5. The footage in Henderson's piece features mesmerising shots of Lake Enriquillo, a lake in the Dominican Republic that often floods due to rises in sea temperature.

V. Select one word for each blank from the following word bank. You may not use any of the words in the bank more than once. Change the form where necessary.

unfortunate	mental	bedfellow	derive	grip
teenager	anorexia	diagnose	therapy	progress

One in six people in the past week experienced a common __1__ health problem, 16 million people in the UK experience a mental illness and know suicide is the biggest killer of men under 45. So with this in mind, you might be forgiven for thinking that mental health and comedy are not easy __2__.

When I was a __3__, I knew nothing about mental health. If you'd have talked about "safe spaces" I'd have thought that you meant a bank. If you'd given a "trigger warning" I'd have thought that was for the benefit of our US friends. And, what's more, I didn't care about mental health. Why would I? Like my dad always used to say, "If it ain't broke, don't fix it!"

But, __4__ my mental health did "break".

Aged 17 I developed __5__. I didn't realize at the time; it was something that developed, rather than "began". It took me a good few years to realize I had a problem, but I never went to get help because I never felt ill enough. When I was 23, I was __6__ as severely clinically anorexic. I had fast-tracked treatment at The Maudsley Hospital in South London and went through 2.5 years of __7__. People are always interested to know what helped me recover and among many things, it was simple: comedy.

I'm a professional stand-up comic. Comedy, for me, began as a hobby and has (unbelievably!) __8__ into a job. One of the things that initially __9__ me about stand up is how it plays with pain. Let me explain.

The word "comedy" is believed to __10__ from the Ancient Greek kōmos meaning "to reveal". It is comedy's job to "reveal" things, to analyze, explain and understand. This was something I turned to when I was in recovery from anorexia. I'd never been able to explain what was going on inside my head; trying to explain what's going on in your mind is like trying to explain a colour to someone who's blind. So, humour became a way of understanding things. Then it became a way of explaining them. Now it's become a way of helping other people. I know I'm not the only one.

Part III Extensive Reading

Text B

Comedy Is in Crisis, No Joke — But Venues and
Comics Are Finding Ways to Fight Back

Comedian Janine Harouni remembers clearly when she first realized that COVID-19 was serious back in March 2020. "The last gig I did, the compere Sophie Duker came out in a hazmat suit and a giant mask, which we all found hilarious. The next day my boyfriend had COVID symptoms. It was a huge reality check."

The London-based New Yorker was nominated for the Edinburgh Comedy Award for

Best Newcomer at the Edinburgh Festival Fringe in 2019. This traditionally kickstarts a career — previous nominees include Tim Minchin and Jimmy Carr. But for Harouni and many other young stand-ups, careers have been on hold.

"It's been a real roller coaster," she says. "Some days I'm like, it's great to have this time to slow down and learn embroidery, and other days I can't get out of bed, and cry because the world's a mess."

Apart from a window when clubs opened for socially distanced shows between lockdowns, this has been a terrible year for live stand-up. Zoom gigs have brought in some much-needed money for performers, but they are no substitute for the thrill of being in the same physical space as the audience.

Michael Odewale was also nominated for the Best Newcomer Award in 2019. The Essex-born stand-up has tried to be optimistic. "It's been strange. Everything screeched to a halt last March and there were obviously low periods where I didn't know what to do next and if my industry could even come back, but there's also been moments of inspiration that come from all that free time such as figuring out how to write sketches and scripts, etc."

While comedians are struggling, at least they are resourceful and have the creative skills to pivot. Harouni has done voiceovers, turning her duvet into a makeshift soundproofed recording booth. Others, such as Richard Herring, have found their voice on the Twitch platform. For venues, life has been tougher. Despite some London clubs receiving grants from the government's £1.57 billion rescue package, the longer the lockdown persists the more likely it is that some may never return.

Islington's Angel Comedy is one of the circuit's most respected spaces. Arena-fillers including John Bishop and Russell Howard have done tour try-outs there. It received £90,425 from the Culture Recovery Fund, but with lockdown ongoing it is not enough to ensure their survival. The venue has looked for other ways to raise money and has just released an online sitcom starring James Acaster and Tim Key that fans can watch by signing up to the venue's Patreon page.

Helen Bauer, another 2019 Best Newcomer nominee, also appears in Angel's webcom. Like many she had to claim Universal Credit as soon as gigs stopped. A survey by the Live Comedy Association, the nearest thing comedy has to a union, found that 27.8% of the industry has been ineligible for any government assistance. Bauer cannot wait to get back on stage. "I was getting ready for Edinburgh 2020 when lockdown happened. Hopefully one day doing festivals will just be part of life again."

One of the problems for stand-up comedy is that it has often been perceived as something of a romantic outsider art. For every Michael McIntyre or Romesh Ranganathan on primetime, there are dozens of aspiring storytellers shuttling between clubs, honing their act. Venues have to be kept going — they're where the future McIntyres and Ranganathans will learn their craft. Nick Mills, who owns 2 Northdown and 21 Soho, agrees:"These kind of venues are paramount, because they've helped develop new talent."

It has been historically hard for the comedy industry to get funding. One performer who spoke off the record told me that the best way to get Arts Council grants in the past was to avoid putting the word "comedy" on your application. Comedy is currently a subcategory of Theatre within the Arts Council's definitions. It is not ineligible but it is not easy getting through the application process. Barry Ferns, who co-founded Angel Comedy says:"It was like writing a dissertation and having to know a whole new subject."

The system is simply not geared to support comedy. But maybe comedy also likes its independence. "It's very cheap and cheerful, we just sort of keep going on a sort of shoestring," says Tamara Cowan, who programmes Camden Comedy Club.

Others, however, feel unsupported. Ryan Taylor, head of comedy at The Pleasance in north London, was frustrated to see clubs who had invested so much into putting COVID protocols in place closed in December, while Christmas shoppers were packed together. "I just feel like we're the easy target."

Odewale also feels let down by the system:"For sure. I think comedy is kind of overlooked and not seen as a legit art form. The process needs to be made easier for comedians and this industry to get the support they need, because people are going to need to laugh when this is over."

So what will the comedy circuit be like when this is over? We hope clubs will survive, but they might well feel different for some time — masks, one-way routes, cabaret seating replacing rows — and capacity reduced while social distancing continues. Personally, I like table service and ordering via app, though it is never going to feel normal when your lager is served by someone in full PPE.

There are positives. A number of people I spoke to talked of continuing to stream gigs now that they have the technology. So fans may well have a choice of watching in person or online. They have also talked of discovering a stronger sense of community. There has been much talk of comedy tackling its own #Me Too issues — the Live Comedy Association is currently involved in addressing that.

The circuit is not going away. As Odewale suggests, the thirst for laughter may be so strong there is a major bounce back. David Armitage, who hosts gigs at Stockwell's Cavendish Arms, adds that comedy does not cave in easily. "Somebody said that this is the death of the arts, or the death of comedy. It's not. It might be the death of some venues, which is awful, but it's not the end of art, music and comedy. It'll be going on somewhere. Try stopping everyone." As for Harouni's boyfriend, you'll be glad to know he is now fine after his early brush with COVID. Let's hope comedy can also make a full recovery.

Total words: 1,072

Total Reading Time: _____ minutes_____ seconds

Vocabulary

hilarious *adj.* 极其滑稽的

nominate *v.* 提名,推荐;任命,指派;挑选,指定(事件的日期或地点)

kickstart *n.* (摩托)脚踏启动板;快速启动

　　　　v. 启动(摩托);开始,重启;振兴

nominee *n.* 被提名人,被任命者

roller coaster *n.* 过山车;不断变化的局势

embroidery *n.* 绣花;刺绣图案;刺绣品

stand-up *adj.* (喜剧节目)单人表演的;激烈的(争论、打斗等);直立的;挺立的

　　　　n. 独角喜剧;单口相声;独白喜剧演员;单口相声演员

screech *v.* 尖叫;尖声地说;发出尖锐刺耳的声音

　　　　n. 刺耳的尖叫,尖锐刺耳的声音

ineligible *adj.* 不合格的;不符合资格的

sitcom *n.* 情景喜剧

aspiring *adj.* 有志成为……的;渴望从事……的

Phrases

fight back 回击;抵抗

gear to 使适合;调整(某物)使其适合……

let down 使失望;辜负;减速下降

Notes

Janine Harouni: Janine Harouni is an actress, writer and New York native living in London. Selected as one of *The Guardian*'s "Ten Comedians to Watch in 2021". Her critically acclaimed debut Edinburgh hour "Stand Up with Janine Harouni (Please Remain Seated)" was nominated for the prestigious Best Newcomer Award at the Edinburgh Fringe. It sold out runs across the UK and US before being filmed as a special for Amazon Prime — available to stream now.

roller coaster: roller coaster is an exciting entertainment in an amusement park, like a fast train that goes up and down very steep slopes and around very sudden bends.

Edinburgh Festival Fringe: The Edinburgh Festival Fringe is the single greatest celebration of arts and culture on the planet. For three weeks in August, the city of Edinburgh welcomes an explosion of creative energy from around the globe. Artists and performers take to hundreds of stages all over the city to present shows for every taste. From big names in the world of entertainment to unknown artists looking to build their careers, the festival caters for everyone and includes theatre, comedy, dance, physical theatre, circus, cabaret, children's shows, musicals, opera, music, spoken word, exhibitions and events.

Universal Credit: Universal Credit is a benefit system that has replaced many older benefits and tax credits. It is for individuals and families of working age, whether they are working or not working.

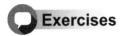 **Exercises**

I. **Answer the following questions after reading the text.**
    1. When did Janine Harouni first realize that COVID-19 was serious?
    2. What award did Michael Odewale receive in 2019?
    3. Does Bauer hopes for getting back on stage?
    4. Why did the performer say the best way to get Arts Council grants in the past was to avoid putting the word "comedy" on your application?
    5. How does Odewale feel about the system?

II. **Decide whether the following statements are true or false according to the text.**
    1. Apart from a window when clubs opened for socially distanced shows between lockdowns, this has been a terrible year for live stand-up.
    2. Michael Odewale was also nominated for the Best Newcomer Award in 2018.
    3. While comedians are struggling, at least they are resourceful and have the creative skills to pivot.
    4. Islington's Angel Comedy is the circuit's most respected spaces.
    5. A survey by the Live Comedy Association, the nearest thing comedy has to a union, found that 27.8% of the industry has been ineligible for any government assistance.

III. **Fill in the blanks with the words given in the brackets. Change the form where necessary.**
    1. The show was_____ (hilarious) — I couldn't stop laughing.
    2. The Security Council can _____ (nominatee) anyone for Secretary-General.
    3. The point of aid was to _____ (kickstarting) business-led growth, not replace it.
    4. Going on a _____ (roller coaster) was a big thrill for everyone.
    5. The shorts had blue _____ (embroidery) over the pockets.
    6. The new rules have made thousands more people _____ (ineligible) for legal aid.
    7. Clare and David Astor are _____ (sketch) a view of far Spanish hills.
    8. Many _____ (aspire) young artists are advised to learn by copying the masters.
    9. I was _____ (fight) back the tears.
    10. Mr. James said he felt _____ (let) down by the show's producers, who allowed him to go on the show.

IV. Translate the following sentences into Chinese.

1. "It's been a real roller coaster," she says. "Some days I'm like, it's great to have this time to slow down and learn embroidery, and other days I can't get out of bed, and cry because the world's a mess."

2. One performer who spoke off the record told me that the best way to get Arts Council grants in the past was to avoid putting the word "comedy" on your application.

3. We hope clubs will survive, but they might well feel different for some time — masks, one-way routes, cabaret seating replacing rows — and capacity reduced while social distancing continues.

4. Comedy is currently a subcategory of Theatre within the Arts Council's definitions. It is not ineligible but it is not easy getting through the application process.

5. One of the problems for stand-up comedy is that it has often been perceived as something of a romantic outsider art.

V. Topics for discussion.

1. How do you understand the differences between comedy and tragedy?
2. Please tell about your favorite comedy.

11 Sports

Part I Pre-reading Questions

1. What kind of sport do you like best and why?
2. What are the benefits of sports for people?
3. In what ways do you think sports can change our country?
4. How do you think of the roles of sports in the digital age?

Part II Intensive Reading

Text A

What Is Medina Spirit's Legacy Following His Sudden Death?
The Answer Is Uncertain

Few horses have had such a short yet newsworthy career as Medina Spirit. And, a day after his sudden death after a workout at Santa Anita, many are wondering how his story will eventually be told.

Will he be the underdog horse that brought trainer Bob Baffert his record-setting 7th Kentucky Derby win? Or will he be the second horse ever disqualified post-race in the 147-year history of the Derby?

Regardless of the outcome, his 3-year-old life started with an unexpected meeting and ended with a tragic and unforeseen outcome.

Up next will be a necropsy, an autopsy performed on animals, which will zero in on the cause of his death Monday morning. Indications point to a cardiovascular event, but in this case, nothing will be left to guesswork.

Scott Chaney, executive director of the California Horse Racing Board, says this might be the most important necropsy the CHRB has ever commissioned, but he says it with a qualification.

"It certainly will be the most scrutinized, but every fatality is important," Chaney said. "Sudden deaths are always more complicated and difficult than musculoskeletal ones."

The body of Medina Spirit was shipped to the UC Davis laboratory in San Bernardino on Monday, while tissue, blood and urine samples were sent to the Maddy Lab at the main campus of UC Davis.

The necropsy will be receiving heightened attention including additional samples sent to labs outside of California, according to Jeff Blea, equine medical director of the CHRB.

"The Maddy Lab is the gold standard in this country, if not the world," Blea said. "So, we are very lucky to have it here. And we will be using multiple departments at Davis to make sure everything is covered. But, we'll also be sending samples out to other labs, just for a second and third set of eyes."

One of those will be at the University of Minnesota, which has a specialty in cardiovascular diagnosis.

While the likelihood is that the initial diagnosis was correct, it's not a certainty. A 2011 study of sudden deaths on almost 300 horses showed that the cause of death was definitively determined in 53% of the cases, and presumed in 25% more. Of the 53% of definitively diagnosed sudden death cases, a cadiovascular or cardiopulmonary cause occurred 56% of the time.

"We just have to rely on the science and the process," Blea said.

There is no timetable for the results, but sudden death necropsies can take two to three months or longer.

Medina Spirit was not the first Kentucky Derby winner to experience sudden death in the same year as his win. In 1984, Swale collapsed and died nine days after winning the Belmont Stakes and a month after winning the Derby. Immediately, there was unfounded speculation of foul play, but it was determined the colt died of heart failure.

While the answers will rest with the science, the future of the sport may well rest with finding a definitive cause of death as the industry and fans wrestle with the loss of one of its biggest stars, albeit one draped in controversy.

Baffert, who told *The Times* on Tuesday that he had nothing to add beyond Monday's statement of "deeply mourning his loss," has talked in the past about the Cinderella stories that can come from racing. Amr Zedan, Medina Spirit's owner, was an owner in search of a miracle when he had an unexpected meeting with Baffert.

"I ran into him at an airport in Dubai on my way to the Saudi Cup," Baffert said in May. "[I hear someone say] 'Hey. Bob,' in the airport and it was him. We sat down there and we just talked for two hours while he was waiting for his flight. He said, 'I was thinking, maybe I'll get back in and maybe we can get together and win the Derby. And I said, 'Yeah, right sure.'"

"Then all of a sudden, he hooked up with Gary Young, the [bloodstock] agent, and Taylor Made [Farm] and Frank Taylor. ... They found this little horse. We looked at him, and, hey, we liked him."

That horse was Medina Spirit, a $35,000 Florida-bred purchase sired by Protonico, whose stud fee was only $5,000. By comparison, Authentic, Baffert's 2020 Kentucky Derby winner, was sired by Into Mischief, who goes for $250,000 a mating. It's partly because of an undervalued sire that Medina Spirit was still in training and not retired after his 3-year-old career such as Authentic. Medina Spirit was being pointed to the San Antonio Stakes on Dec. 26 at Santa Anita. The goal was to run him in the $20-million Saudi Cup on Feb. 26 in Saudi Arabia.

After the horse started training, he was gaining more attention than such a low purchase horse normally gets.

"I have him down at Los Alamitos," Baffert recalled. "My assistant down there says, 'You know that horse they didn't give much for? I think he's OK.' And sure enough he broke his maiden."

Medina Spirit won five of his 10 lifetime races including the Grade 1 Awesome Again and, of course, the Kentucky Derby. His last race was a second in the Breeders' Cup Classic running against older horses. He earned a little more than $3.5 million.

He was an unexpected winner of the Kentucky Derby, with most of the prerace attention going to Essential Quality, Hot Rod Charlie and Rock Your World. Medina Spirit went to the lead and was expected to give it up in the stretch of the 1-mile race, but he wouldn't yield.

"He's a fighter," said his jockey John Velazquez in May. "I know he was going to fight anybody who would come to him. Every time I asked him for more, he kept going more and more. That's all you can ask for a horse."

The jubilation of the Derby win was loud and long until a week later when Baffert was informed that the colt tested positive for betamethasone, a legal anti-inflammatory that is not allowed on race day. What has ensued has been challenges to the testing, challenges to the rules, lots of lawyers, and a Kentucky Horse Racing Commission that still has not set a hearing for Baffert or addressed the idea if Medina Spirit will remain the winner of the Kentucky Derby.

How this plays out, and how Medina Spirit is remembered, will most likely be decided by scientists and lawyers. How the public will view things is much more complicated.

Total words: 1,080

Total Reading Time: _____ minutes _____ seconds

💬 Vocabulary

newsworthy *adj.* 有新闻价值的

indication *n.* 表明,标示;象征,显示

qualification *n.* (通过考试或学习课程取得的)资格,学历;资历,限定条件

cardiovascular *adj.* [医] 心血管的

scrutinize *v.* 仔细查看,细致审查

fatality *n.* (战争、事故中的)死亡；致命性；宿命

tissue *n.* 纸巾，手巾纸；（动物或植物的细胞的）组织；薄纸

specialty *n.* 专业，专长；特色菜，特产

diagnosis *n.* 诊断，判断

presume *v.* 假设，设想；（法律上或官方）假定，推定

collapse *v.* 倒塌，坍塌；崩溃，瓦解；倒下，昏倒；突然贬值，暴跌

　　　　n. 倒塌，塌陷；突然失败，崩溃；病倒，垮掉

jubilation *n.* 欢欣鼓舞；欢腾；欢庆

heighten *v.* 提高，加强

Phrases

rely on 依靠，依赖

foul play 严重犯规；不公平的比赛；不正当行为

make sure 确信；证实

Notes

Medina Spirit: Medina Spirit, the winner of the 2021 Kentucky Derby, collapsed and died after a routine workout on Monday morning at the Santa Anita racetrack in Southern California.

The Times: *The Times* is a daily newspaper published in London, one of Britain's oldest and most influential newspapers. It is generally accounted, with *The Guardian* and *The Daily Telegraph*, one of Britain's "big three" and has long been recognized as one of the world's greatest newspapers.

Kentucky Derby: the most prestigious American horse race, established in 1875 and run annually on the first Saturday in May at Churchill Downs racetrack, Louisville, Kentucky.

Dubai: the most populous city in the United Arab Emirates (UAE). It is located on the southeast coast of the Persian Gulf and is one of the seven emirates that make up the country.

Exercises

I. Answer the following questions after reading the text.

　　1. What happened to the horse Medina Spirit?

　　2. What are the achievements of Medina Spirit?

3. How was the of necropsy of Medina Spirit conducted?

4. Was Medina Spirit the first Kentucky Derby winner to experience sudden death in the same year as his win?

5. How does the author see the answers for Medina Spirit's death?

II. Decide whether the following statements are true or false according to the text.

1. Few horses have had such a short yet newsworthy career as Medina Spirit.

2. Regardless of the outcome, his 3-year-old life started with an unexpected meeting and ended with a tragic and unforeseen outcome.

3. Scott Chaney, executive director of the California Horse Racing Board, says this might not be the most important necropsy the CHRB has ever commissioned, but he says it with a qualification.

4. There is no timetable for the results, but sudden death necropsies can take two to three years or longer.

5. In 1984, Swale collapsed and died nine days after winning the Belmont Stakes and a month after winning the Derby.

III. Fill in the blank of the following sentences with one of the words or phrases given below. Change the form where necessary.

| special | collapse | diagnose | jubilation | fatal |
| newsworth | qualify | presume | indicate | scrutinize |

1. The number of deaths makes the story _____.

2. A survey of retired people has _____ that most are independent and enjoying life.

3. We _____ for the final by beating Stanford on Tuesday.

4. Her purpose was to _____ his features to see if he was an honest man.

5. It would be _____ for the nation to overlook the urgency of the situation.

6. In addition to great skewers, grilled seafood is the _____ here.

7. The soldiers were _____ as having flu.

8. We must _____ innocence until we have proof of guilt.

9. The governor called for an inquiry into the motorway's _____.

10. I read the note and was filled with joy and _____.

IV. Translate the following sentences into Chinese.

1. Few horses have had such a short yet newsworthy career as Medina Spirit. And, a

day after his sudden death after a workout at Santa Anita, many are wondering how his story will eventually be told.

2. "It certainly will be the most scrutinized, but every fatality is important," Chaney said. "Sudden deaths are always more complicated and difficult than musculoskeletal ones."

3. There is no timetable for the results, but sudden death necropsies can take two to three months or longer.

4. Medina Spirit was not the first Kentucky Derby winner to experience sudden death in the same year as his win. In 1984, Swale collapsed and died nine days after winning the Belmont Stakes and a month after winning the Derby.

5. How this plays out, and how Medina Spirit is remembered, will most likely be decided by scientists and lawyers. How the public will view things is much more complicated.

V. Select one word for each blank from the following word bank. You may not use any of the words in the bank more than once. Change the form where necessary.

division	impact	cope with	consist	massive
negative	tap into	foundation	revolution	pressure

Sport has been ___1___ by many different strands of science and that is certainly the case where psychology is concerned.

___2___ the power of the mind has become increasingly prominent in sport, with clubs and organizations eager to try and maximize the performance of their athletes.

Modern sport is certainly a __3__ environment, with factors such as scrutiny from the media and fan demands sometimes taking a big toll on competitors.

Mistakes can also be a major issue for athletes, particularly when their performances can affect punters' chances of winning on live betting markets or __4__ impact the finances of clubs.

Read on as we take a look at the origins of sports psychology and assess how it has changed sport in the United Kingdom.

The rise of sports psychology

Psychology has long been known to be a factor in sport, but it wasn't until the 1920s that the subject was researched in any depth.

However, that work laid the __5__ for countries such as Russia and the United States to throw proper resources at studies around 30 years later.

The UK followed suit during the 1960s, with the newly-formed British Society of Sports Psychology driving big advances in the research.

Now part of the British Association of Sport and Exercise Sciences (BASES) organisation, the Psychology __6__ is widely renowned as a leader in its field.

O'Sullivan highlights sports psychology's importance

Snooker star Ronnie O'Sullivan has been a shining example of the importance of sports psychology with regards to performance.

The five-time world champion is supremely talented, but his health and well-being have suffered as he struggles to __7__ depression and the demands placed on him by the sport.

His decision to consult Dr. Steve Peters, who had worked with the British cycling squad at the 2008 Olympics, helped him ease what he once described as "a treadmill of turmoil".

Although his moods can still fluctuate __8__, O'Sullivan's career has undoubtedly been elongated as a result of him embracing the power of sports psychology.

Football embracing a new way of thinking

Andy Hill has spent the past five years working as a sports psychologist with the players, coaches and staff at Championship club Blackburn Rovers.

He says that improving a coach's ability to shape behaviour is important, helping the players become more __9__ performers and have better relationships with their coaches.

Hill also spends time working on team dynamics, improving communication and building up a "common goal" ethic amongst the playing squad.

His efforts have clearly had a positive __10__ on the club, with Rovers currently challenging for a return to the Premier League after an eight-year absence.

Part III　**Extensive Reading**

Text B

Powerlifter Karenjeet Kaur Bains Wants to
Inspire More Women to Take up Strength Sports

Karenjeet Kaur Bains started her sporting life as a sprinter, but when she took up powerlifting at the age of 17 — initially to get faster and more explosive for athletics — her focus soon changed.

"I found a love for feeling strong and never looked back" is how Bains explains the switch of sports.

Under the guidance of her father, a former bodybuilder and powerlifter, she quickly displayed her prowess in the squat, bench press and deadlift. Three months later, she entered — and won — her first ever competition.

Fast-forward eight years and Bains now holds the accolade of being the first Sikh woman to compete for Great Britain in powerlifting.

Her "ultimate dream", she says, is to be the first Sikh female world champion, as well as using her platform to inspire other girls to take up the sport.

"Strength sport is often such a male-dominated sport," Bains tells CNN. "You get the stereotype that you're going to turn into Arnold Schwarzenegger with a wig on, or something like that ... it would be a dream for me to have girls like me coming up the ranks in the juniors and they look like me and you never saw them before."

Bains started powerlifting when she was 17 and entered her first competition a few months later.

Bains, a regional 300-meter sprint champion as a teenager, found sporting inspiration throughout her family when she was growing up.

Her older twin brothers were national level 400-meter hurdlers, and she recalls watching them fly around the track "like Superman".

Her mother, meanwhile, was encouraged to take up athletics by Bains' father and won local championship medals in the hammer throw, discus, and shot put in her 40s.

"She had always wanted to do sport when she was younger, but she never got a chance because she came from Punjab, India, and back then, girls didn't have the same chances to do sports and education," says Bains of her mother.

"Her older brother was a champion wrestler in India as well, but she couldn't, and I think she always wanted to do something sporty."

"My parents never stopped me, they always pushed me equally," she adds. "I've had role models everywhere, really."

Bains' father, Kuldip Singh Bains, is a former bodybuilder and powerlifter.

Having helped with her training during her time in athletics, Bains' father has also been her coach throughout her powerlifting career.

On top of passing on the wisdom he accumulated during his own career, he's also helped build a gym at the family home in Warwickshire, England, which is where Bains does much of her training today.

"It's quite raw and rustic. It's nothing fancy," she says. "My dad's an engineer and he's made a lot of the machines and the weights and everything, so it's all been done by hand.

"We have a really fantastic relationship. Obviously, my dad always says he considers himself a dad first and then a coach second ... it's really nice how it almost developed quite from the grassroots — when I was a schoolgirl with a dream — all the way to the international stage. And I did this with my dad."

Bains' home gym includes equipment built by her father.

One of the highlights of Bains' powerlifting career so far, she says, was a gold medal in the junior division at the 2019 Commonwealth Powerlifting Championships.

In October, she competed as a senior lifter for the first time at the World Bench Championships in Vilnius, Lithuania, placing sixth and equaling her competition best of 92.5 kilograms (almost 204 pounds).

Her focus is now on training throughout the winter in preparation for the national championships at the start of next year.

But improving on her biggest lifts and winning more titles is just one of Bains' powerlifting goals.

"I became the first British Sikh female to go to the world championships for Great Britain, but then I don't want to be the last," she says.

"I want this to open the gates for many more diverse people, not just Sikh people, anybody from a minority, diverse background who might not have had a chance."

During her career, Bains hopes to inspire more diverse participation in strength sports.

Bains' religion forms an important part of her sporting career.

She chooses to compete under her full name and include the traditional Sikh name Kaur because it serves as "a reminder to carry yourself in higher regard, to be a good person, to help people," she explains.

Each time she walks onto the stage at competitions, Bains takes time to remember God's name and reflect on the hardships she's overcome.

"If it wasn't for my faith, I think I would not have been as mentally honed in ... it definitely helps me channel focus in a positive way," she says.

According to a report released in 2018 by Sporting Equals — a charity promoting equality, diversity and inclusion in sport and physical activity — which engaged 194 South Asian women in the UK, 74% of respondents claimed to be inactive and undertook less than

30 minutes of physical activity per week.

The report also found that South Asian women in the UK are more likely than men to be inactive.

In acknowledging some of the entry barriers South Asian women can face in sport, Bains says: "I think the issue is often in our culture — you need to focus on your academics, get a good job, don't want any distractions. And often, they see that if you pursue things outside of academics, which might be a distraction."

"That might be one of the reasons that some girls don't do it or they just don't see enough role models. I've always hoped to get my message out there ... because I think if you see someone who's done it, you can use that as an example and follow suit."

As part of promoting that message, Bains visits schools and posts regularly about her powerlifting career on social media.

Her life can be busy. Bains is an ambassador for Brawn — a global, community app for strength athletes created to bring together and connect anyone interested in strength training — and also has had to juggle training with work as an accountant given her powerlifting career isn't centrally funded.

While taking her accountancy exams, most days would involve getting up at 6 a.m. and going to bed at 1 a.m., in between which she would fit studying and going to the gym around her day job in London.

"There were never enough hours in the day for me," says Bains. But it all seems worthwhile when she gets sent messages saying she inspired someone to go the gym or take up a new sport. "If I know I'm helping someone out there or giving them a spark of motivation," she adds, "then I did a good job."

Total words: 1,153

Total Reading Time: _____ minutes _____ seconds

Vocabulary

powerlifting *n.* 力量举重
explosive *adj.* 易爆炸的，可能引起爆炸的；突增的，爆炸性的；暴躁的
　　　　n. 炸药，爆炸物
accolade *n.* 荣誉；赞扬；表扬；奖励
championship *n.* 锦标赛；冠军地位
wrestler *n.* 摔跤运动员
stereotype *n.* 模式化观念，老一套；刻板印象
　　　　v. 对……形成模式化的看法
division *n.* 分开，分配；除法；部门；分歧，不和；分界线
athletic *adj.* 健壮的；体育运动的

inclusion *n.* 包含，包括；被包括的人（或事物）

distraction *n.* 使人分心的事物，使人分心的事；消遣，娱乐

accountant *n.* 会计，会计师

motivation *n.* 动力，诱因，动机

juggle *v.* 玩杂耍

　　　　v. 尽力同时应付

academic *adj.* 学业的，学术的；学校的，学院的

　　　　n. 高等院校教师；高校科研人员

Phrases

follow suit 跟着做；学样

reflect on 仔细考虑，思考；反省

in preparation for 为……做准备

Notes

powerlifting: Powerlifting refers to a strength sport. The whole point of the sport is to find out just how strong you really are. The basics are incredibly simple. In competition, a powerlifter stands alone on a platform and tries to lift the heaviest weights he is capable of for a single repetition.

Great Britain: Great Britain is located to the northwest of continental Europe and to the east of Ireland. The North Sea and the English Channel separate it from Europe. The Channel Tunnel, the longest undersea rail tunnel in the world, connects it with continental Europe.

Sikh: Sikh is developed in Punjab in the late 15th century and is based on a belief that there is only one God.

Hammer throw: Hammer throw is a sport of strength, balance, and projection. Apart from heavy physical strength, it requires excellent foot work coordination. Since 1900, it is a part of Olympic Games in men's category.

Exercises

I. **Answer the following questions after reading the text.**

　1. When did Karenjeet Kaur Bains start her sporting life as a sprinter?

　2. Under whose guidance did Bains display her talents in this area?

　3. What is Bains' "ultimate dream"?

4. What did her father do to help her?

5. How is her life except for being an athlete?

II. Decide whether the following statements are true or false according to the text.

1. Karenjeet Kaur Bains started her sporting life as a sprinter, but when she took up powerlifting at the age of 17 her focus soon changed.

2. Under the guidance of her mother, a former bodybuilder and powerlifter, she quickly displayed her prowess in the squat, bench press and deadlift.

3. Her older brother was a champion wrestler in India as well, but she couldn't, and I think she always wanted to do something sporty.

4. One of the highlights of Bains' powerlifting career so far, she says, was a gold medal in the senior division at the 2019 Commonwealth Powerlifting Championships.

5. Each time she walks onto the stage at competitions, Bains takes time to remember God's name and reflect on the hardships she's overcome.

III. Fill in the blanks with the words given in the brackets. Change the form where necessary.

1. Don't get me wrong, _____ (powerlift) takes a lot of skill, I'm just saying that there is more athleticism involved in weightlifting.

2. He's inherited his father's _____ (explode) temper.

3. The Nobel Prize has become the ultimate _____ (accolade) in the sciences.

4. She's won the _____ (championship) three years running.

5. There's always been a _____ (stereotype) about successful businessmen.

6. The funds needed will mainly be drawn from _____ (accumulate) within the enterprise.

7. Mark Spitz was a great _____ (athletic).

8. This will cost money, but if social _____ (include) is to succeed, it must be spent.

9. Tom admits that playing video games sometimes _____ (distract) him from his homework.

10. They are _____ (motivate) by a need to achieve.

IV. Translate the following sentences into Chinese.

1. Under the guidance of her father, a former bodybuilder and powerlifter, she quickly displayed her prowess in the squat, bench press and deadlift. Three months later, she entered — and won — her first ever competition.

2. Her mother, meanwhile, was encouraged to take up athletics by Bains' father and

won local championship medals in the hammer throw, discus, and shot put in her 40s.

3. One of the highlights of Bains' powerlifting career so far, she says, was a gold medal in the junior division at the 2019 Commonwealth Powerlifting Championships.

4. "I want this to open the gates for many more diverse people, not just Sikh people, anybody from a minority, diverse background who might not have had a chance."

5. While taking her accountancy exams, most days would involve getting up at 6 a.m. and going to bed at 1 a.m., in between which she would fit studying and going to the gym around her day job in London.

V. Topics for discussion.
1. Conduct a survey on people who do sports in your class.
2. What are the similarities between doing sports and reading?

Unit 12 Technology

Part I Pre-reading Questions

1. What do you know about Facebook?
2. What companies do you know have ever changed their names?
3. Why do some companies change their names?
4. What's your opinion on McDonald changing its name to "Golden Arches" in China?

Part II Intensive Reading

Text A

Facebook Is Changing Its Name to Meta as It Focuses on the Virtual World

In a 75-minute online presentation, CEO Mark Zuckerberg urged users to adjust their thinking about the company, which he said had outgrown its ubiquitous and problematic social media app — a platform that will continue to be known as Facebook. Instead, he said, the company plans to focus on what Zuckerberg described as the next wave of computing: a virtual universe where people will roam freely as avatars, attending virtual business meetings, shopping in virtual stores and socializing at virtual get-togethers.

"From now on, we're going to be the metaverse first. Not Facebook first," Zuckerberg said at Connect, the company's annual event focused on virtual and augmented reality. "Facebook is one of the most-used products in the world. But increasingly, it doesn't encompass everything that we do. Right now, our brand is so tightly linked to one product that it can't possibly represent everything we are doing."

The move comes as Facebook is mired in controversy over allegations that it has privately and meticulously tracked real-world harms exacerbated by its platforms, ignored warnings from its employees about the risks of their design decisions and exposed vulnerable communities around the world to a cocktail of dangerous content. After a whistle-blower this month turned over tens of thousands of internal company documents to Congress and the US Securities and Exchange Commission, lawmakers and critics have called for urgent action to rein in the tech giant.

The revelations by whistle-blower Frances Haugen represent arguably the most profound challenge yet to Zuckerberg and his company, which ranks as the largest social media platform in the world. Critics swiftly criticized the move, comparing it to the crisis strategy employed by tobacco company Phillip Morris when it became clear that the company had long known that cigarettes damage human health.

"Don't forget that when Phillip Morris changed [its] name to Altria it was still selling cigarettes that caused cancer," tweeted Democratic lawyer Marc Elias.

Zuckerberg said the rebrand would heed the "lessons" of the past, noting in a blog post that privacy and safety would be built into the new generation of products "from Day One" — a clear nod to Facebook's record of eroding trust. In his keynote address, he also nodded to Facebook's problems, saying, "The last few years have been humbling for me and my company in a lot of ways."

Harbath noted that roughly every five years, the company has announced a big directional change amid a bad press cycle. In 2012, the company pivoted to mobile while getting attacked for a poor performance during its public offering.

For the time being, Facebook's name change seems aspirational. A company that Zuckerberg launched from a college dorm room 17 years ago has become a conglomerate encompassing WhatsApp, Instagram, Messenger and a nascent payments and hardware business, leading some experts and insiders to say that the company was long overdue for a name change.

But virtually all of Facebook's revenue — $29 billion in the third quarter — comes from online advertising produced by the core blue Facebook app, meaning that any transition to virtual reality focused on the sale of hardware would take enormous investment and many years.

"While the name change indicates a larger vision, that transformation is not yet a reality and will be a years-long investment," eMarketer analyst Audrey Schomer said in an email.

Zuckerberg and Facebook have acknowledged that. Zuckerberg said in his keynote that the process to become a metaverse company would take a "decade" and that his goal was for it to "reach a billion people" over that time. On Monday, the company said its investments in the metaverse — which include a commitment to hiring 10,000 new people in hardware jobs — will shave $10 billion off its 2021 profits.

Zuckerberg's keynote was filled with a dizzying array of scenes that showcased the company's vision for the metaverse. It included Zuckerberg doing his favorite water sport, hydrofoiling, with friends in a virtual environment, and then jumping into work meetings from a virtual home office, boxing with virtual avatars and working out on a virtual lily pad.

In a letter on the company's website posted shortly after the keynote, Zuckerberg said that the future would be "an embodied Internet where you're in the experience, not just looking at it. We call this the metaverse, and it will touch every product we build."

Zuckerberg began talking about how the company would transition to a new identity this summer. He subsequently announced a smart-glasses partnership with Ray-Ban and a plan to use its virtual reality headsets for work-related videoconferencing. He promoted a longtime friend who heads the hardware division, Andrew Bosworth, to become the company's new chief technology officer.

The political dimension of the rebrand also began months before Haugen emerged with the Facebook Papers. Facebook executives spent parts of the summer introducing the metaverse idea to experts in Washington think tanks and planning outreach to federal agencies that might regulate its hardware, The Post previously reported. Zuckerberg has told colleagues that he no longer wants to be the face of the company's headaches in Washington and elsewhere.

Facebook also isn't the first Silicon Valley company to rebrand itself. Google changed its parent company's name to Alphabet in 2015 in an attempt to unify a corporate behemoth that encompassed not only search-and-display advertising but also driverless cars and a life-sciences division. Snapchat changed its name to Snap Inc. in an attempt to rebrand itself as a camera company.

Zuckerberg said that the name "meta" was inspired by his love of the classics, and that it comes from the Greek word "beyond".

"For me, it symbolizes that there is always more to build, and there is always a next chapter to the story."

Total words: 975

Total Reading Time: _____ minutes _____ seconds

🗨 Vocabulary

outgrow *v.* 长得穿不下（衣服）；增长得容不进（某地）；比……长得高

avatar *n.* （神的）化身（印度教和佛教中化作人形或兽形的神）

get-together *n.* 聚会，联欢会

encompass *v.* 包含；包围，包括；涉及

allegation *n.* （无证据的）说法，指控

meticulously *adv.* 细致地；一丝不苟地

exacerbate *v.* 使加剧；使恶化

cocktail *n.* 混合物；鸡尾酒

whistle-blower *n.* （公司等处）检举揭发舞弊内情的人

rebrand *v.* 重塑……的形象

disinformation *n.* 虚假信息；假消息

aspirational *adj.* 渴望成功的；一心想提高社会地位和生活水平的

conglomerate *n.* 企业集团；聚合物

nascent *adj.* 新生的；萌芽的；未成熟的

showcase *n.* （商店、博物馆等的）玻璃柜台

hydrofoil *n.* 水翼船

behemoth *n.* 巨头（指规模庞大、实力雄厚的公司或机构）

Phrases

be mired in 陷入……困境中

turn over 移交

rein in 控制；约束

shave off 削减

Notes

metaverse: The metaverse is a collective virtual shared space, created by the convergence of virtually enhanced physical reality and physically persistent virtual space, including the sum of all virtual worlds, augmented reality, and the Internet.

augmented reality: Augmented reality (AR) is an enhanced version of the real physical world that is achieved through the use of digital visual elements, sound, or other sensory stimuli delivered via technology. It is a growing trend among companies involved in mobile computing and business applications in particular.

Securities and Exchange Commission: The US Securities and Exchange Commission (SEC) is an independent federal government regulatory agency responsible for protecting investors, maintaining fair and orderly functioning of the securities markets, and facilitating capital formation. It was created by Congress in 1934 as the first federal regulator of the securities markets.

Exercises

I. **Answer the following questions after reading the text.**

1. According to Mark Zuckerberg, what does the company intend to center around in the coming years?

2. Why does the company decide to change its name from Facebook to Meta?

3. What is the biggest source of income for the company?

4. According to Zuckerberg, how long will it take the company to turn itself into a metaverse company?

5. What are some of the measures the company has taken to facilitate the transition?

II. Decide whether the following statements are true or false according to the text.

1. According to Mark Zuckerberg, users' idea of the company is no longer proper.

2. The Facebook platform will be renamed as Meta.

3. Facebook has been the priority of the company until now.

4. According to some experts and insiders, the rebrand comes just in time.

5. Andrew Bosworth used to be chief of the company's hardware division.

III. Fill in the blank of the following sentences with one of the words or phrases given below. Change the form where necessary.

cocktail	aspirational	allegation	rebrand	behemoth
showcase	nascent	exacerbate	outgrow	conglomerate

1. Indian Railways will present a display _____ its achievements in the past 150 years.

2. I'm afraid I will have to crush your dreams and creative _____, for your own good.

3. Such behavior is part of the process of a _____ democracy; it could and should be seen as a hopeful sign.

4. His comments were ignored by the media as he did not have the proof to back up his _____.

5. He was _____ his graphic design company and moving premises to a new €2.3 million site in Donnybrook.

6. People could not evaluate the true risk of their investments because financial _____ were distorting market signals.

7. Guilt, selfishness, deep sorrow and frustration all mingled together in my conscience like a deadly _____.

8. To set the scene, the company had been growing quite quickly over the preceding few years, and had already _____ the 2-year-old purpose-built headquarters.

9. These issues were all being felt in our local communities, with the last three years of public housing reforms only _____ the situation.

10. Small, independent broadcasters cannot possibly compete with media _____ controlling 40% or more of the market share in any given city.

IV. Translate the following sentences into Chinese.

1. In a 75-minute online presentation, CEO Mark Zuckerberg urged users to adjust their thinking about the company, which he said had outgrown its ubiquitous and problematic social media app — a platform that will continue to be known as Facebook.

2. Right now, our brand is so tightly linked to one product that it can't possibly represent everything we are doing.

3. Zuckerberg said the rebrand would heed the "lessons" of the past, noting in a blog post that privacy and safety would be built into the new generation of products "from Day One" — a clear nod to Facebook's record of eroding trust.

4. A company that Zuckerberg launched from a college dorm room 17 years ago has become a conglomerate encompassing WhatsApp, Instagram, Messenger and a nascent payments and hardware business, leading some experts and insiders to say that the company was long overdue for a name change.

5. In a letter on the company's website posted shortly after the keynote, Zuckerberg said that the future would be "an embodied internet where you're in the experience, not just looking at it".

V. Select one word for each blank from the following word bank. You may not use any of the words in the bank more than once. Change the form where necessary.

transition	segment	tracking	signal	resemble
livestreamed	iconic	interact	encompass	rebrand

In a move that __1__ the company's growing focus on augmented and virtual hydrofoiling projects, Facebook — which owns the photo sharing app Instagram, the virtual reality company Oculus and the messaging platforms Messenger and WhatsApp, as well as its namesake social network — will now be known as Meta.

The new name is a nod to the idea of the "metaverse", a concept trendy in Silicon Valley that __2__ a mix of physical, virtual and mixed realities that users can access and __3__ with through devices such as virtual reality headsets or mixed-reality glasses.

"I believe the metaverse is the next chapter for the Internet, and it's the next chapter for our company, too," said Mark Zuckerberg, Facebook's founder and chief executive, during a Thursday morning media event.

Zuckerberg's announcement came a little over an hour into a __4__ Facebook Connect keynote event. Before the reveal, Zuckerberg and other company leaders discussed a variety of metaverse projects the company is working on, including work and exercise simulations, real-time virtual __5__ of physical objects and photorealistic online avatars.

This __6__ has been a long time coming for Zuckerberg. After acquiring Oculus for $2 billion in 2014, he described virtual reality as "the future of computing".

Zuckerberg acknowledged on Thursday that the __7__ — and the corporate vision it embodies — is a shift in focus from the social media realm that defined Facebook's early days. But he said the company's driving goal — connecting people — remains the same.

"The metaverse is the next frontier, just like social networking was when we got started," Zuckerberg said. Facebook, he added, "is one of the most used products in the history of the world. It is a/an __8__ social media brand. But increasingly, it just doesn't encompass everything that we do."

The company is now "looking at and reporting on" its business as "two different __9__ ", he added: a "family of apps" on one hand and "future platforms" on the other.

The company's apps and their branding will remain the same. The "What We Build" section of the newly updated Meta website still lists a Facebook app — that is, the flagship social network — underneath a banner featuring the Meta umbrella company's new logo, which __10__ an infinity sign.

Part III　Extensive Reading

Text B

The Metaverse Is Coming and It's a Very Big Deal

Imagine walking down the street. Suddenly, you think of a product you need.

Immediately next to you, a vending machine appears, filled with the product and variations you were thinking of. You stop, pick an item from the vending machine, it's shipped to your house, and then continue on your way.

Next, imagine a husband and wife. The husband offers to go to the store but the wife can't remember the name and type of product she needs. Her brain-computer interface device recognizes it for her and transmits a link to her husband's device, along with what stores and aisles it's located in.

Welcome to the metaverse, alternate digital realities where people work, play, and socialize. You can call it the metaverse, the mirror world, the AR Cloud, the Magicverse, the Spatial Internet, or Live Maps, but one thing is for certain, it's coming and it's a big deal.

Google the term "metaverse" and you'll find several definitions. Wikipedia defines it as a collective virtual shared space, created by the convergence of virtually enhanced physical reality and physically persistent virtual space, including the sum of all virtual worlds, augmented reality, and the Internet. The word "metaverse" is a portmanteau of the prefix "meta" (meaning beyond) and "universe"; the term is typically used to describe the concept of a future iteration of the Internet, made up of persistent, shared, 3D virtual spaces linked into a perceived virtual universe.

Currently, you can only experience the Internet when you go to it, but with new connectivity, devices and technologies, we'll be able to experience it all around every single day.

More than just a term from a Neal Stephenson sci-fi novel, the metaverse is being built today. *Wired*'s Kevin Kelly wrote a cover story in 2019 titled "Welcome to the Mirrorworld". In it, he describes how augmented reality will spark the next big tech platform. In essence, "we are building a 1-to-1 map of almost unimaginable scope. When it's complete, our physical reality will merge with the digital universe." In other words, get ready to meet your digital twin, and the digital twin of your house, your country, your office, and even your life.

Today, the metaverse is a shared virtual space where people are represented by digital avatars (think *Ready Player One*). The virtual world constantly grows and evolves based on the decisions and actions of the society within it. Eventually, people will be able to enter the metaverse, completely virtually (*i.e.* with virtual reality) or interact with parts of it in their physical space with the help of augmented and mixed reality.

Leslie Shannon, Nokia's Head of Trend Scouting, referred to the importance of the metaverse, or spatial Internet, in a recent talk during the VRARA's Global Summit. During her talk she stated that, "The spatial Internet is the culmination of everything that AR and VR is developing today. It's the idea of taking information about things, locations, or historical events and actually locating that information out there in the world where it's most relevant." Augmented reality and virtual reality will be the ways you will see this information layer.

Marketing and communications professionals need to pay attention to the metaverse because it's the next frontier for online interaction. Just like social media revolutionized the online marketing landscape, so too will the metaverse. While we don't have one shared metaverse at this time, there are companies positioning working on creating it.

Fortnite, Minecraft, and Animal Crossing are games now but they already have big user bases, detailed worlds, and user-generated content. Facebook is also positing itself towards the metaverse with its virtual reality social media platform, Horizon (currently in beta), and Live Maps. Niantic, Magic Leap, Microsoft and many others are working on it too.

The pandemic too has shifted culture online. Family reunions on Zoom, weddings relocated to Animal Crossing, graduations on Minecraft and virtually trying on clothes have all become common practices. With online social gatherings becoming more mainstream and online video games increasing their world-building, "it's inevitable that brands will play a significant role in the metaverse."

Economy

Companies will need to transition their marketing strategies from online ad buys to existing in a shared, virtual economy. Companies will need to do market research on their new customers in the metaverse. How people act and what their preferences are in the metaverse could be totally different than how they behave and what they shop for in real life.

While there are sure to be ads in the metaverse, brands can actually be part of creating the metaverse itself. Brands should approach this with responsibility and ethics and not make our world one giant ad. This is of the utmost importance.

Culture

Digital clothing, world-building, or marketing can have a real impact on brands. In the metaverse, people won't be individually wandering around. They will have friendships, relationships (with autonomous NPCs, holograms or other people) who will affect their decisions. Brands will need to continue adapting to relationship styles of play and interactions. Customers won't just be able to talk to brands like on social media, they'll be able to interact with them in 3D form.

Shopping

Online shopping is a given in the metaverse. But it's more than digitally trying on clothes people can purchase for real life. Virtual fashion, avatar "skins", and virtual real estate (housing, cars, etc.) will have their own worth in the metaverse. Companies will have to design brands for different people at different stages of wealth. People who invest heavily in the metaverse may have their own businesses and property, therefore partner opportunities with businesses that don't exist in physical reality.

Fashion is a big part of creating a character or being represented by an avatar. Virtual fashion houses and designers have a chance to enter a whole new market of digital-first clothing. The metaverse is about identity in ways that haven't been possible before.

Entertainment

In Fortnite, real-world celebrities play the game and players become celebrities themselves. In the metaverse, brands won't be able to hide behind the scenes with pre-made ads, commercials, and products. They themselves will have to be personable and approachable. People will go to brands in the metaverse because they feel a connection, not necessarily a need for that product or service.

A huge opportunity

Are you ready for the opportunities the metaverse will bring?

A new iteration of the Internet is being worked on and this will have massive implications for society. Marketing, communications, and branding professionals will face new challenges but also new opportunities. This new era of the metaverse will unleash amazing creativity and open up new frontiers and horizons for brands and businesses. Now the question is, how are you getting ready?

Total words: 1,118

Total Reading Time: _____ minutes _____ seconds

Vocabulary

variation *n.* 变化, 变更; 变体

interface *n.* 界面

transmit *v.* 传送; 传输

metaverse *n.* 虚拟世界; 元宇宙

convergence *n.* 趋同; 汇集, 相交

persistent *adj.* 连绵的; 持续的; 反复出现的

portmanteau *n.* 两格式旅行衣箱
　　　　　 adj. 综合的; 复合式的

iteration *n.* 迭代; 新版软件

connectivity *n.* 连接 (度), 联结 (度)

spatial *adj.* 空间的

culmination *n.* 顶点; 巅峰

hologram *n.* 全息图

celebrity *n.* 名人, 名望; 名誉

unleash *v.* 发泄; 突然释放

Phrases

vending machine 自动贩卖机, 自动售货机

cover story 封面故事 (杂志中与封面图片有关的内容)

in beta 处于测试中

Notes

Neal Stephenson: Neal Stephenson (born October 31, 1959) is an American science-fiction writer with a deep love for the arts. From a young age, Stephenson was fond of coming up with stories, and once he went full-time into writing, he has never stopped. Neal Stephenson is the writer who coined the term "metaverse" 30 years ago in his novel "Snow Crash."

Wired: *Wired* is a monthly American magazine, published in print and online editions, that focuses on how emerging technologies affect culture, the economy, and politics. Owned by Condé Nast, it is headquartered in San Francisco, California, and has been in publication since March or April, 1993.

Ready Player One: *Ready Player One* is a 2011 science fiction novel, and the debut novel of American author Ernest Cline. The story, set in a dystopia in 2045, follows protagonist Wade Watts on his search for an Easter egg in a worldwide virtual reality game, the discovery of which would lead him to inherit the game creator's fortune. In the novel, Wade Watts has an avatar named Parzival.

Exercises

I. **Answer the following questions after reading the text.**

1. According to the text, what can be assured about the metaverse?
2. According to the text, how will the Internet be different in the future?
3. Who first used the word "metaverse"?
4. According to Leslie Shannon, what would today's AR and VR bring finally?
5. According to the text, what influence does COVID-19 have on our culture?

II. **Decide whether the following statements are true or false according to the text.**

1. We can infer from the first paragraph that people in the metaverse can pick a drink from the virtual vending machine and immediately drink it.
2. The meaning of the word "metaverse" is clear and definite.
3. The word "metaverse" first appeared in a sci-fi novel.
4. According to Kevin Kelly, our physical reality will be replaced by the digital universe.
5. For the time being, people still don't have a common metaverse.

III. **Fill in the blanks with the words given in the brackets. Change the form where necessary.**

1. And of course the announcements were largely _____ (iterate) of existing products and/or concepts.

2. Also, left-handed men and women are likely to have less well-developed _____ (space) awareness, suggesting that they may be more prone to accidents such as car crashes.

3. Viral _____ (pandemic) occur with surprising regularity throughout world history.

4. The packages have to be very light and the measuring device has to produce an electrical signal which can be _____ (transmit) by radio.

5. One of Linux's greatest assets is its ability to add value to legacy technology investments by connecting and _____ (interface) with old equipment or software.

6. A _____ (hologram) image of a scientist walked across the courtroom toward Raven's bench and spoke loudly so that all in the room could hear him.

7. The more choice we have, the less likely we are to enjoy the shared experience — unless it's wandering around the supermarket _____ (aisle) in a mass daze, wondering what to buy.

8. The school student may be too naive to know that karaoke is a _____ (portmanteau) word blending two Japanese words:"kara" meaning empty (as in karate meaning empty hand) and oke (short for okesutora meaning orchestra).

9. The arrest is the _____ (culminate) of an investigation which has been ongoing for upwards of 18 months.

10. The low-density surface water moved shoreward over the upwelled water, forming a _____ (converge) zone at the front.

IV. Translate the following sentences into Chinese.

1. Her brain-computer interface device recognizes it for her and transmits a link to her husband's device, along with what stores and aisles it's located in.

2. Wikipedia defines it as a collective virtual shared space, created by the convergence of virtually enhanced physical reality and physically persistent virtual space, including the sum of all virtual worlds, augmented reality, and the Internet.

3. In essence, "we are building a 1-to-1 map of almost unimaginable scope. When it's complete, our physical reality will merge with the digital universe."

4. Eventually, people will be able to enter the metaverse, completely virtually (*i.e.* with virtual reality) or interact with parts of it in their physical space with the help of augmented and mixed reality.

5. The spatial Internet is the culmination of everything that AR and VR is developing today. It's the idea of taking information about things, locations, or historical events and actually locating that information out there in the world where it's most relevant.

V. Topics for discussion.
    1. How do you think Metaverse will impact college students?
    2. What should we do to be better prepared for the Metaverse?

Unit 13 Climate and Environment

Part I **Pre-reading Questions**

1. In what way is human health influenced by climate change?
2. How much do you know about 2021 United Nations Climate Change Conference (COP26)?
3. Are all the countries around the world equally impacted by climate change?
4. How much do you know about today's young people in Africa?

Part II **Intensive Reading**

Text A

Effort to Reframe Climate Change as a Health Crisis Gains Steam

For the first time at a major United Nations Climate Conference, human health is emerging as a leading issue, a reframing that brings climate change's far-reaching and long-lasting effects to the forefront.

Although health has been addressed at conferences going back to the first UN Environmental Summit in 1992, never before has it held such a central role. The 2015 Paris Accord, the global agreement among nations to reduce greenhouse gas emissions, was billed foremost as a historic environmental moment.

However, "the Paris Agreement is not an environmental treaty," said Dr. Maria Neira, the director of the World Health Organization's department on environment, climate change and health. "It is a basic public health treaty."

There is a growing body of research showing that climate change is contributing to a wide range of health risks around the world. It is exacerbating heat waves, intensifying wildfires, heightening flood risks and worsening droughts. These are, in turn, increasing heat-related mortality, pregnancy complications and cardiovascular disease. And as with

164

many things climate-related, the risks and harms are particularly severe in places that are the least able to respond.

There is also a cascade of indirect health consequences that threaten to unravel decades of progress on improving water quality and food security. Drier soil can contribute to malnutrition. Warming temperatures and changing humidity levels can expand habitats suitable to dengue- or malaria-carrying mosquitoes, lyme-carrying ticks, and the pathogens that cause diseases like cholera and Valley Fever.

At the same time, two years of grappling with the coronavirus pandemic has underscored to politicians the importance of health as a national and global priority.

For reasons like these, the health community has strategized that if it can make people the face of climate change — rather than traditional environmental icons, such as polar bears or forests — political leaders may be more inclined to take action.

In the months leading up to the Glasgow conference, known as COP26, the world's leading public health organizations, medical journals and professional organizations released a series of reports and editorials placing health at the heart of the climate issue. One letter signed by organizations representing 47 million global health professionals declared the climate crisis "the single biggest health threat facing humanity." The World Health Organization estimates that between 2030 and 2050, at least 250,000 additional deaths will occur every year as a result of climate change.

In one sign of the emphasis placed on health this year, 15 countries, including Ireland and Mozambique, have already made significant pledges to decarbonize their national health systems.

"This year represents a quantum leap in how health is being covered at COP," said Josh Karliner, the international director of program and strategy at Health Care Without Harm, an organization that has worked to reduce the health care sector's environmental footprint.

Around the world, health care providers have said that they are already seeing the effects of climate change on their patients, as well as on the ability of hospitals to continue providing care during extreme weather. At the same time, there has been a growing awareness of the health care sector's own contribution to greenhouse gas emissions.

Hospitals around the world have been hit hard by extreme weather and are increasingly grappling with the reality that they weren't designed for the intensity of storms, heat and other challenges that are becoming more commonplace. Floods killed COVID patients at a hospital in Mexico. Hospitals in India suffered severe flooding. As wildfires burned on the West Coast, hospitals struggled to maintain their indoor air quality. A hurricane ripped the roof of a rural Louisiana hospital.

During the Pacific Northwest heat wave this summer, Dr. Jeremy Hess, a professor of emergency medicine at the University of Washington, was working in the emergency department at Harborview Medical Center, the highest-level trauma center for several states. Dr. Hess has worked in emergency departments during mass casualty events, but the heat wave stuck out.

"It was more sustained," he said. "It was an environmental emergency that wasn't stopping."

For days, patients came in with third-degree burns on their feet from walking on hot asphalt, he said. Many succumbed to heat-related death before even making it to the hospital. Doctors scrambled to have body bags filled with ice on gurneys.

Hospitals across the region were stressed in other ways. Providence, a large health care organization in the West, had no spare beds at their emergency departments spanning the northern part of Washington State down to southern Oregon. One hospital closed its psychiatric unit to ensure there was adequate power in more critical parts of the building.

That week, more than 1,000 heat-related emergency visits were reported in the Pacific Northwest, compared with fewer than 10 visits during the same period in 2019. Researchers found that such an intensive heat wave would have been virtually impossible without the influence of human-caused climate change.

Doctors say they have also seen the health effects of a changing climate in their day-to-day interactions with patients.

For years, Dr. Renee Salas, an emergency medicine doctor at Massachusetts General Hospital, said that she has noticed allergy seasons are lasting longer, stressing her patients with asthma and lung diseases. She thought climate change may be behind it — and science has borne out her suspicions. Studies have found that since 1990 pollen seasons have not only become longer but also contain higher pollen concentrations, and that climate change is a driving factor.

"I think about climate change as a secondary diagnosis in my patients," said Dr. Salas, a co-author of *The Lancet Countdown*, a report on climate change and health.

The health burdens are unlikely to be shared equally.

In September, a report from the Environmental Protection Agency found that although all Americans will be affected by climate change, minorities are likely to face more health risks. Black Americans, for instance, are 40% more likely to live in areas with the highest increases in mortality due to extreme temperature.

"The same vulnerable communities that were disproportionately hurt by COVID-19 are bearing disproportionate harm from climate change," Dr. John Balbus, the interim director of the US Department of Health and Human Services' Office of Climate Change and Health Equity, wrote in an email.

Meanwhile, there's been growing recognition within the health industry of its own contributions to climate change.

It is estimated that the health care sector accounts for close to 5% of all global carbon dioxide emissions. Some of that comes from powering energy-intensive hospitals and clinics 24 hours a day, but the majority — an estimated 70% — is related to its supply chain and the energy required to produce, ship and dispose of the machines, pharmaceuticals and equipment used every day.

Over the past decade, 43,000 hospitals and health centers in 72 countries have signed on as members of the Global Green and Healthy Hospitals, a network of organizations aimed at reducing their environmental impact.

"It is a trend," said Alison Santore, the chief advocacy and sustainability officer for Providence, the hospital chain, which is a member of the green-hospital group. "But it's still the minority of hospitals when we look at the whole."

Total words: 1,185

Total Reading Time: _____ minutes_____ seconds

Vocabulary

accord *n.* 协议，条约

　　　v. 符合；一致

drought *n.* 干旱，旱灾

mortality *n.* 死亡数量，死亡率

malnutrition *n.* 营养不良

humidity *n.* 潮湿，湿气；湿度

dengue *n.* 登革热

malaria *n.* 疟疾

tick *n.* 蜱，壁虱，扁虱（吸血寄生虫，有些种类能传播疾病）

grapple *v.* 扭打；搏斗

underscore *v.* 强调；画底线标出

　　　n. 底线

decarbonize *v.* (使)……碳减排；清除……的碳沉淀

trauma *n.* 创伤；痛苦经历

casualty *n.* 伤员；亡者；受害者

asphalt *n.* 沥青；柏油

scramble *vt.* 艰难地（或仓促地）完成

gurney *n.* (医院用来移动病人的) 轮床

allergy *n.* 过敏反应，过敏症

asthma *n.* 哮喘

pollen *n.* 花粉

　　　v. 授粉

disproportionately *adv.* 不成比例地

pharmaceutical *adj.* 制药的

　　　n. 药物

Phrases

gain steam 迅速增长；逐渐强大

bill sb./sth. as sth. 把（某人或事物）宣传为……

pregnancy complication 妊娠并发症

a cascade of 大量，许多（像瀑布一样）

quantum leap 突变；巨变；飞跃

succumb to 屈服于……

body bag 运尸袋

Notes

Lyme disease: Lyme disease is a bacterial infection you get from the bite of an infected tick. At first, Lyme disease usually causes symptoms such as a rash, fever, headache, and fatigue. But if it is not treated early, the infection can spread to your joints, heart, and nervous system. Prompt treatment can help you recover quickly.

Valley Fever: Valley Fever is a disease caused by a fungus (or mold) called Coccidioides. The fungi live in the soil of dry areas like the southwestern US. You get it from inhaling the spores of the fungus. The infection cannot spread from person to person. It can make you feel like you have a cold or influenza (flu) and may cause a rash. Most people get better without treatment.

COP26: COP26 is the 2021 United Nations Climate Change Conference. For nearly three decades the UN has been bringing together almost every country on earth for global climate summits — called COPs — which stands for "Conference of the Parties". In that time climate change has gone from being a fringe issue to a global priority. This year will be the 26th annual summit — giving it the name COP26. With the UK as President, COP26 takes place in Glasgow.

Exercises

I. **Answer the following questions after reading the text.**

1. What is the purpose of the 2015 Paris Accord?

2. According to some researches, what harms are being done to the world by the climate change?

3. What has made the politicians begin to attach greater importance to human health?

4. According to the health community, what may better prompt action from political leaders?

5. How does climate change make asthma and lung diseases worse?

II. Decide whether the following statements are true or false according to the text.

1. According to the text, the United Nations climate conference has never before addressed the health problem.

2. The harms and risks caused by the climate change are equally severe all around the world.

3. We can infer from the text that traditional environmental icons are not effective in promoting political leaders to take action.

4. According to Josh Karliner, COP of this year is a big progress in addressing health problems.

5. The communities that were disproportionately hurt by COVID-19 are less hurt by climate change.

III. Fill in the blank of the following sentences with one of the words or phrases given below. Change the form where necessary.

underscore	allergy	mortality	disproportionately	decarbonize
accord	grapple	drought	scramble	trauma

1. This machine can _____ any petrol engine.

2. Older cars contribute _____ to global warming.

3. Chinese officials say cloud seeding has helped to relieve severe _____ and water shortages in cities.

4. His family is struggling and _____ to deal with not only the emotional issues but the financial impact as well.

5. Symptoms of a food _____ usually develop within about an hour after eating the offending food.

6. The two of them then _____ and fell on to the sofa but during the struggle he grabbed the purse and fled.

7. In 1996, peace _____ were signed to bring an end to the armed conflict and to strike at the root causes of war.

8. The most dramatic and perhaps most significant cause of natural _____ among gray whales is predation by killer whales.

9. The research _____, for example, the importance of people's being motivated to become a part of the host culture, of having a strong sense of self and of finding a cultural mentor.

10. She has a dark, dark secret that would twist the mind of any cat that has experienced the _____ she has, and seen the things she's seen.

IV. Translate the following sentences into Chinese.

1. For the first time at a major United Nations Climate Conference, human health is emerging as a leading issue, a reframing that brings climate change's far-reaching and long-lasting effects to the forefront.

2. The 2015 Paris Accord, the global agreement among nations to reduce greenhouse gas emissions, was billed foremost as a historic environmental moment.

3. There is also a cascade of indirect health consequences that threaten to unravel decades of progress on improving water quality and food security.

4. Hospitals around the world have been hit hard by extreme weather and are increasingly grappling with the reality that they weren't designed for the intensity of storms, heat and other challenges that are becoming more commonplace.

5. Some of that comes from powering energy-intensive hospitals and clinics 24 hours a day, but the majority — an estimated 70% — is related to its supply chain and the energy required to produce, ship and dispose of the machines, pharmaceuticals and equipment used every day.

V. Select one word for each blank from the following word bank. You may not use any of the words in the bank more than once. Change the form where necessary.

account	channel	disruption	outnumber	hazard
security	severity	combat	result	release

While we know now that the threat of violent attacks from domestic sources

____1____ those from foreign sources, a bigger source of insecurity still is that of climate change. On October 21, the DHS ___2___ its first-ever "Strategic Framework for Addressing Climate Change", acknowledging the importance of climate as a source of ___3___ and threat to security. As the COP26 UN Climate Meetings start this week, it's time for a recognition that climate change is in fact a more expensive, more deadly, and more real threat to lives and to the US economy than the threat of what we call terrorism.

Instead of wasting trillions of dollars and millions of lives fighting a war on terror, the US should be mobilizing to ___4___ climate change. Federal spending should be ___5___ toward clean energy projects, other decarbonization efforts, and adaptation for a changing climate. The increase in extreme weather events has already cost the US hundreds of billions of dollars in weather-related damages and the frequency and ___6___ of these types of events will only increase unless swift and sweeping actions are taken. Climate-related disasters have killed more Americans from flooding and wildfires than the 2,996 people who died in the 9/11 attacks. Wildfires have ___7___ in over 3,200 deaths in the US since 2000, according to recent research in *The Lancet*. Hurricane Katrina alone killed over 1,800 people in 2005. *The Atlas of Mortality* from the World Meteorological Organization finds that the US ___8___ for 38% of global economic losses from caused by weather, climate, and water ___9___.

It's time for the US to shift toward the biggest threat to our ___10___, and to direct federal resources accordingly.

Part III　Extensive Reading

Text B

Young Climate Activists Warn Their Elders: Stop Destroying the Planet

After the cops showed up in an urban forest and detained Manisha Dhinde, one of them asked her: "What is this fashion of protesting for the environment?"

"It isn't fashion," Dhinde snapped back on that day two years ago. "It is my duty to save trees."

She was opposing plans to cut down 2,700 trees in order to build a metro train car shed on tribal land in Mumbai. That moment galvanized the petite woman with the deep voice, and now she is aiming to work with marginalized communities across her state of Maharashtra to stop or at least reshape development projects that would harm the environment.

"We don't respect anyone more than we respect nature," Dhinde, 22 years old, said of the tribes living on shrinking green space in this traffic-congested, air-polluted city.

Dhinde is part of a surge of young environmentalists determined to stave off climate change by challenging the destructive ways of their elders. In Uganda, a climate activist who once worked in her family's battery supply shop has found international fame for bringing Africa and the Global South into the conversation. In Scotland, a woman who quit college to warn of rising temperatures and a troubling carbon footprint is battling politicians and corporations she accuses of attempting to co-opt and distort the climate change movement.

All three are part of the first generation to come of age at a time when the effects of the climate crisis are already being felt — foreshadowing a perilous future. Their fight is propelled by the technology they have mastered: unparalleled access to information and to one another — thousands of miles but only milliseconds apart on the social media platforms that have heralded their cause.

Their confrontational strategy is reminiscent of the young antiwar and civil rights protesters of the 1960s. But the existential stakes are much higher today. Disillusioned by economic and political designs that have long favored big industry and fossil fuels over the environment, this generation faces the prospect that entire regions of the world will become increasingly uninhabitable. Their TikTok videos and social media scrolls are a kaleidoscope of climate refugees, sinking cities, parched farmlands and endangered wildlife.

"The planet is warming, the animals are disappearing, the rivers are dying, and our plants don't flower like they did before," Txai Suruí, a 24-year-old indigenous climate activist from the Brazilian Amazon, told world leaders on the opening day of the United Nations COP26 summit in Glasgow, Scotland, this week. "The Earth is speaking. She tells us that we have no more time."

By any measure, the outlook is grim. Oceans are hotter than they've ever been and the rate of sea level rise has doubled since 2006. Carbon dioxide levels in the atmosphere haven't been this high in 2 million years. More than 1 million plants and animal species are at risk of extinction. No matter what changes are made today, the young will inherit a planet that over the next 30 years will see worsening heat waves, droughts and flooding, according to a recent United Nations report. The effects of greenhouse gas emissions, it said, are "irreversible for centuries to millennia".

The impact will be most profound for the young in poorer countries. In Africa, where the population is growing at twice the rate as in South Asia or Latin America, and is expected to double by 2050, the number of youths being born into a warming climate is booming. Almost half of the populations of many African countries, including Niger, Mali, Uganda and Congo, are under age 15. Those young are already living through the crisis. Cyclones have torn through the south; desert locusts have endangered the food supply in the east; the Nile River's water supply is unsteady.

"It's not the devastation that keeps us fighting. It's what we see in our minds — the vision, the hope," said Vanessa Nakate, an activist from Uganda. "Because if there's no hope, what are we to look forward to?"

Nakate was having trouble falling asleep in her sweltering attic bedroom in Kampala. It was 2018, and so hot and dry, farmers had noticed their yields were suffering. Then came the floods. Nakate watched in horror as rising waters and landslides in eastern Uganda drove 21,000 people from their homes. More than 50 people died, including children buried in the mud of an elementary school.

It seemed extreme weather events were becoming more frequent and lasting longer. She asked her Uncle Charles whether she was imagining things. He told her that the world was in trouble.

Nakate was shy and introverted. She worried she would be mistaken for a prostitute if she staged a one-woman protest at a busy Kampala intersection. But compelled to act, she enlisted her siblings and cousins and made posters: Nature is life; climate strike now; thanks for the global warming. So nervous she couldn't feel her legs, she uploaded photos of their six-person strike to Twitter. Thunberg retweeted them, and Nakate's act of defiance went viral.

A college graduate with a business degree, Nakate became a rare African voice in a chorus of young climate change activists. In early 2020, she was in Davos, Switzerland, sleeping in a tent despite subzero temperatures to prove an energy-efficient point during the World Economic Forum. But it was her skin color, not her environmentalism, that made her famous when she was trimmed out of a photograph with four white activists.

"They hadn't just cropped me out, I realized," she said. "They'd cropped out a whole continent."

That moment of humiliation in the Alps steeled her. She quickly emerged as a leading critic on the disproportionate impact of climate change on the Global South, or poorer regions outside of North America and Europe. The average person in Uganda, like other African countries, emits less carbon dioxide in a year than a person in the United Kingdom does in just two weeks, she said, but they are the first to face extreme economic loss and forced migration.

The rate of sea level rise in countries like Madagascar is above average; more than half of the coastlines of Benin, Togo, Ivory Coast and Senegal are eroding; and thanks to extreme heat and flooding, disease-carrying mosquitoes are inhabiting new altitudes of the East African highlands. In some regions of Africa, the number of undernourished people has increased by almost 50% in the last decade.

Total words: 1,088

Total Reading Time: _____ minutes _____ seconds

Vocabulary

detain *v.* 拘留,扣押

tribal *n.* (尤指南亚的)部落成员
　　adj. 部落的,部族的

galvanize *v.* 使震惊;激励;刺激

petite *adj.* (女孩、妇女或身材)娇小的,纤弱的

marginalized *adj.* 被边缘化的

congested *adj.* 拥挤的;挤满的

co-opt *v.* 拉拢;笼络;增选

foreshadow *v.* 预示;是……的预兆

perilous *adj.* 危险的,艰险的

propel *v.* 推进,驱动;推进

unparalleled *adj.* 无比的;无双的;空前的

testify *v.* (尤指出法庭上)作证;证明,证实

admonish *v.* 责备;告诫;警告

confrontational *adj.* 对抗性的;挑起冲突的

reminiscent *adj.* 使人回忆起(人或事);缅怀往事的

disillusion *v.* 使醒悟,使不再抱幻想;使理想破灭

kaleidoscope *n.* 万花筒;千变万化

parched *adj.* 焦干的;晒焦的;干渴的

irreversible *adj.* 不可逆的;无法复原的;不能倒转的

sweltering *adj.* 闷热的

attic *n.* 阁楼,顶楼

introverted *adj.* 内向的

prostitute *n.* 卖淫者,娼妓

sibling *n.* 兄弟姐妹

undernourished *adj.* 营养不良的,营养不足的

 Phrases

snap back 厉声回应

stave off 避开;延缓

be reminiscent of 让人联想到;令人想起

go viral 快速传开,走红

Notes

Global South: The Global South is a term often used to identify lower-income countries on one side of the so-called divide, the other side being the countries of the Global North (often equated with developed countries). As such, the term does not inherently refer to a geographical south; for example, most of the Global South is geographically within the Northern Hemisphere.

carbon footprint: According to WHO, a carbon footprint is a measure of the impact your activities have on the amount of carbon dioxide (CO_2) produced through the burning of fossil fuels and is expressed as a weight of CO_2 emissions produced in tons.

desert locust: A desert locust is a type of grasshopper — but far more devastating than the common garden variety. Locusts are part of a large group of insects commonly called grasshoppers. However, locusts differ from grasshoppers in that they have the ability to change their behavior and habits and can migrate over large distances. They can form swarms, which can be dense and highly mobile and can then fly as much as 150 km a day, given favorable winds. These swarms can devour large amounts of vegetation and crops.

Exercises

I. **Answer the following questions after reading the text.**
   1. Why are over 2,000 trees planned to be cut in Mumbai?
   2. According to Dhinde, what do they have the greatest regard for?
   3. What does "a kaleidoscope of" mean according to the text?
   4. What will our planet be like in 30 years according to the text?
   5. What does "They'd cropped out a whole continent." mean?

II. **Decide whether the following statements are true or false according to the text.**
   1. We can learn from the text that Mumbai has bad traffic and poor air.
   2. The confrontational strategy adopted by today's young climate activists is totally different from that adopted by the young antiwar and civil rights protesters of the 1960s.
   3. According to the text, sea level didn't rise until 2006.
   4. People around the world suffer from climate change to the same extent.
   5. Of all the African countries, Uganda emits the least carbon dioxide each year.

III. **Fill in the blanks with the words given in the brackets. Change the form where necessary.**
   1. There has been a very huge difference between actually arresting someone and _____ (detain) him for questioning.

2. It came in 1990, undermining their magnanimity, but also _____ (galvanize) me and my colleagues into human rights activism.

3. Many of them said there was no reason to wear a seat belt because most of the streets in the city were so _____ (congest) with traffic.

4. After all, what Hollywood screenwriter would spend half an hour _____ (foreshadow) an event that never arrives?

5. He does just that and embarks on the most _____ (peril) journey of his life.

6. The sudden rise in unemployment is _____ (parallel) in the post-war period.

7. If you know your business like a book, _____ (testify) as an expert witness can be a lucrative sideline.

8. In addition, clients are _____ (admonish) to drink at least two quarts of water each day to help cleanse the body of toxins associated with weight loss and exercise.

9. I thought that I had removed it when I became _____ (illusion) by the whole process.

10. The future effects are unknown, but drug experts fear they may include _____ (reverse) brain damage or mental illness.

IV. Translate the following sentences into Chinese.

1. Their fight is propelled by the technology they have mastered: unparalleled access to information and to one another — thousands of miles but only milliseconds apart on the social media platforms that have heralded their cause.

2. Disillusioned by economic and political designs that have long favored big industry and fossil fuels over the environment, this generation faces the prospect that entire regions of the world will become increasingly uninhabitable.

3. In Africa, where the population is growing at twice the rate as in South Asia or Latin America, and is expected to double by 2050, the number of youths being born into a warming climate is booming.

4. It's not the devastation that keeps us fighting. It's what we see in our minds — the vision, the hope.

5. The average person in Uganda, like other African countries, emits less carbon dioxide in a year than a person in the United Kingdom does in just two weeks, she said, but they are the first to face extreme economic loss and forced migration.

V. Topics for discussion.

1. What can we do to help curb the climate change?
2. How can we strike a balance between economic development and environmental protection?

Unit 14 Social Problems

Part I **Pre-reading Questions**

Part I   Pre-reading Questions

1. What do social problems refer to? Please list some prevailing social problems in the world.
2. At present, lots of traditions have been commercialized. What do you think of such commercialization?
3. What's the purpose of practicing yoga in your opinion?
4. How should we curb spams and nuisance phone calls in an effective way?

Part II   Intensive Reading

Text A

How Western Society Has Commercialized Yoga

Western societies have turned this 5,000-year-old spiritual practice into a product — what can we do about it?

In July, 2020, Sweaty Betty announced that they would be changing the names of some of their activewear products, responding to Internet criticisms calling out the cultural appropriation and commercialization of yoga. These product names previously featured sacred Sanskrit words and greetings, which Sweaty Betty said, "Separated from their sacred foundations ... felt insensitive" and they "felt it was inappropriate to sell products using these culturally important words".

The announcement was generally met with praise. Many applauded Sweaty Betty for taking steps to address their appropriation. However, Western societies' commercialization of yoga remains an issue with a once sacred spiritual practice now estimated to be worth $80 billion worldwide.

The origins of yoga can be traced back some 5,000 years to Northern India where its purpose was to train the body and mind in self-observation and awareness. The word "yoga" comes from the Sanskrit root "yuj", meaning "to unite" and its goal was to unite the body, mind and soul.

While yoga itself is not a religion, the two are deeply connected, its origins stemming from Hinduism and being used in multiple other religious practices. For Minreet Kaur, a henna artist and journalist from West London, yoga is heavily entwined with her faith as a Sikh. "I like to do some form of yoga daily with meditation. I can chant Waheguru — meaning 'wonderful God' — and it gives me peace of mind and cleanses the body."

She explains:"The Sikh prayer Gurbani states that the highest form of yoga is meditation. For a Sikh to achieve liberation or union with God, one must remain absorbed in meditation upon the Lord's name; this is the best way of yoga."

The typical Western perception of yoga, however, is radically different. When we think of yoga, we conjure up images of slim, tanned, blonde women in Lululemon leggings doing sun salutations on the beach. We think of state-of-the-art studios with "namaste" painted on the walls in fancy script. We think of social media influencers with Om tattoos sharing pictures of perfectly posed handstands to their thousands of Instagram followers.

While yoga has eight limbs of practice; guidelines on how to live a purposeful life, Western interpretations often focus on just one — asana or the physical practice — represented in the media by toned, white, model-like bodies. This glamorized form is a far cry from the practice's origins and our image-based culture has reduced a sacred spiritual practice into "a fashionable form of physical exercise with a touch of Eastern exoticism" that the West is massively profiting from.

Rina Deshpande, Ed.M., MS.T., ERYT-500, is a first-generation Indian-American yoga and mindfulness researcher, writer and teacher, and was raised with yoga as part of the teachings of her culture and Indian roots. She speaks about the use of Sanskrit scriptures on clothing. "When something becomes a tattoo or a print on a shirt, it risks being tokenized as a trendy foreign design." Her parents, on the other hand, can read Sanskrit and truly embody the words. She says, "People who are buying yoga merchandise may not understand that it's not just pretty but rather carries deep meaning. Seeing my parents illuminates the difference between commercial branding and authenticity."

An example of such is namaste, which is printed on everything from tank tops to posters. This traditional Hindu greeting has a literal meaning of "the god in me bows to the god in you" and is typically used at the end of a yoga class to acknowledge the divine in each other. Put into context, and it feels incredibly insensitive to print a word of such hefty religious meaning on a commercial product, stripping it of its cultural significance.

And, as this glamorized version of yoga's popularity grows, we're finding more and more ways to profit from it and straying further away from its original meaning. One development over the past few years is "brewga", a class that marries "the joy of drinking beer and mindfulness of yoga" in one practice.

Shilpa Panchmatia, a London-based business growth coach questions the intentions of people choosing to attend these classes, asking, "Do people come to do yoga? Or, do they come to socialize?" She talks about how alcohol is frowned upon in many of the religions that practice yoga and claims, "[having the practice] and alcohol together shows disrespect towards these religions."

Rina explains that this commercialization exploits yoga's sacred origins. "Am I in favour of drinking beer while doing yoga? I think that just means that it's not yoga and I wish the name yoga wasn't taken for it."

In the West, the way yoga has been marketed to us means that many of us have adopted a cultural practice without acknowledging its true meaning, turning it into a fashionable workout. Does that mean we shouldn't do yoga? Not necessarily, but we do need to be more mindful in our practice to avoid harmful appropriation. Rina wants to invite people to reflect and educate themselves on the origins and true meaning of the practice. She explains, "Appropriation can feel like you're not really seeing the culture. Yes, we can all practice yoga but let's acknowledge where it came from."

We need to respect the lineage we have the privilege of accessing instead of just consuming the parts we find attractive. And by doing that, we can truly begin to access the healing power that yoga can offer.

Total words: 985

Total Reading Time: _____ minutes _____ seconds

🎧 Vocabulary

commercialize v. 商业化；利用……牟利

activewear n. 运动服

appropriation n. 挪用，占用；拨款

sacred adj. 神的，神圣的；受尊重的；受崇敬的

Sanskrit n. 梵文

insensitive adj. 未意识到的；漠不关心的；懵然不知的，麻木不仁的

Hinduism n. 印度教

entwine v. 缠绕，盘绕

meditation n. 冥想；沉思，深思

chant v. 唱圣歌；反复唱，反复呼喊
　　　 n. 圣歌，重复唱的歌词

cleanse v. 清洁；净化；清洗

perception n. 看法，感知；洞察力

salutation n. 招呼，致意的动作；(信函、演讲开头的)称呼语

namaste n. 合十礼

script n. 剧本，讲稿；笔迹

limb *n.* 肢，臂，翼；腿

asana *n.* 瑜伽体位

exoticism *n.* 异国情调；外国风情

mindfulness *n.* 正念

tattoo *n.* 文身

tokenize *v.* 装饰，标记

embody *v.* 具体表现，体现；收录，包括

illuminate *v.* 照明；阐明

authenticity *n.* 真实性，确实性

Hindu *n.* 印度教教徒

hefty *adj.* 大而重的，沉重的；猛烈的

strip *n.* (纸、金属、织物等)条，带
　　　v. 除去，脱衣；剥夺；拆卸

glamorize *v.* 美化，使有魅力

stray *v.* 走失，迷路；走神，离题

lineage *n.* 家系；血统；世系

Phrases

call out 唤起；呼吁；召集

stem from 源于

be entwined with 与……缠绕在一起

conjure up 使……呈现于脑际；用咒语使……出现

frown upon 不赞成；反对

Notes

Sweaty Betty: Sweaty Betty is a British retailer specializing in women's activewear, founded by Tamara and Simon Hill-Norton. In August, 2021, Sweaty Betty was bought by American apparel manufacturer Wolverine Worldwide.

Instagram: Instagram refers to an American photo and video sharing social networking service founded by Kevin Systrom and Mike Krieger.

Exercises

I.　**Answer the following questions after reading the text.**

1. What issue would be addressed in the announcement of Sweaty Betty?

2. What was the purpose of original yoga?

3. What does the writer want to illustrate by citing Minreet Kaur's statement?

4. What does "authenticity" refer to in the context of "Seeing my parents illuminates the difference between commercial branding and authenticity."?

5. According to the writer, how should we treat it in a right way when we commercialize yoga?

II. **Decide whether the following statements are true or false according to the text.**

1. Many people frowned upon the announcement of Sweaty Betty.

2. Westerners generally treat yoga as a trendy way of physical exercise.

3. When consumers are buying yoga products, they may not be clear about the underlying meaning of using Sanskrit scriptures on clothing.

4. According to the text, we can learn that the "brewga" was a typical example to embody the true culture behind yoga practice.

5. According to the text, it is inferred that the writer was in favor of Rina's viewpoints.

III. **Fill in the blank of the following sentences with one of the words or phrases given below. Change the form where necessary.**

| commercialize | appropriation | sacred | insensitive | authenticity |
| perception | strip | entwine | meditation | exoticism |

1. In fact, the history of caricature has often been _____ with the history of censorship.

2. Unlike the first time, when traveling to Mexico was something of an _____ journey to a foreign land, his return was more akin to a homecoming.

3. The paper should have established the _____ of the documents before publishing them.

4. The man was then _____ of his gold medal and condemned by the media and public.

5. The museum itself has been designed to merge with the local architecture and contains artifacts that are both _____ and secular.

6. As the monk _____ in silence, his mind cleared and his self-centered thoughts faded away.

7. Well, the only thing is she is so extraordinarily responsive and _____ to any move that he make that it's uncanny.

8. It is wise to never underestimate human _____ and the ability of the person on the end of the line to sense attitudes.

9. Stealing _____ the fruits of someone else's labor without his permission.

10. The manager needs to get them involved in an economic agenda where they can see the results of their labour _____.

IV. Translate the following sentences into Chinese.

1. While yoga itself is not a religion, the two are deeply connected, its origins stemming from Hinduism and being used in multiple other religious practices.

2. When we think of yoga, we conjure up images of slim, tanned, blonde women in Lululemon leggings doing sun salutations on the beach.

3. When something becomes a tattoo or a print on a shirt, it risks being tokenized as a trendy foreign design.

4. And, as this glamorized version of yoga's popularity grows, we're finding more and more ways to profit from it and straying further away from its original meaning.

5. In the West, the way yoga has been marketed to us means that many of us have adopted a cultural practice without acknowledging its true meaning, turning it into a fashionable workout.

V. Select one word for each blank from the following word bank. You may not use any of the words in the bank more than once. Change the form where necessary.

inevitable	expert	stigma	benefit	work
embarrass	legal	remove	lock	mutual

When going through a divorce, it can be difficult to speak to your friends and the people around you about what's going on.

It can even feel ___1___, which it shouldn't. Normalizing talk about divorce is something that society needs to head towards. After all, divorces usually end up being better for both individuals involved.

Accepting the reality

The more you are able to open up and talk to people, the easier it will be to accept the situation.

Whether it's a ___2___ divorce or one-sided, accepting what is happening will be the best way for you to move on. Don't keep things ___3___ down to yourself, if you don't feel comfortable yet to speak to people around you, then consider speaking to a therapist.

Therapy is a fine way to help deal with issues you've got buried down deep inside, but you'll know what's best for you.

Learning about the process

It has gotten to the point in our society that people just don't know how the process of divorce ___4___.

This makes it harder to deal with and talk about. People simply don't know how to listen to divorce talk or, therefore, talk about it.

So, let's spend some time explaining the process for when you need to sort out a divorce.

When getting a divorce, the first thing you need to do is find an attorney to work with. They will not only be on your side to represent you ___5___ to get the best, but they will handle all the paperwork and explain what's happening.

When finding your lawyer, you should focus your attention onto family law firms. These specialize within these departments so you know that your needs are looked after in an ___6___ fashion. If you live in Houston, TX, then consider looking into divorce law firms in the area.

Fullenweider Wilhite are one such divorce law firm in Houston, TX, who can advise you with more information. They explain all on their website about what services they offer, so you can see what works for you.

Once you're going through the process, you'll understand it a lot more.

Ending the stigma

At the end of the day, we really need to ___7___ the stigma surrounding a divorce. It is, after all, a very common event. There are plenty of reasons as to why a relationship would end in a divorce, and mostly it's for the ___8___ of both people.

Even if the divorce was rough, after enough time has passed, everything will work out. That's ___9___. Choosing to take a divorce a few decades ago was unthinkable in society, especially for women. It was really seen as a patriarchal thing that they had no say in.

I imagine as you read that you thought that was a really silly point, and that's where we should take the ___10___ of modern divorces.

If modern divorces right now are in a state of judgment and embarrassment, then hopefully it won't take too long until people view them in the same way as divorces in the 50s. Outdated stigma needs to go.

Part III   Extensive Reading

Text B

Sometimes Talking, Not Tech, Is the Answer to Social Problems

At the grand old age of 33, I am (just) old enough to remember teenage life before mobile phones. Instead, one of my friends had a pager, and to reach her you had to phone an operator and dictate a message. Profanity was prohibited. I have a distinct memory of telling a call centre worker that, yes, I did want to refer to my friend as a "stupid bar steward".

My point is that teenagers are creative, and, when it suits them, determined. That's why I winced when Jeremy Hunt called for tech companies to ban under-18s from "sexting" — sending explicit messages through smart phones. It felt like he was setting teenagers a challenge.

"There is a lot of evidence that the technology industry, if they put their mind to it, can do really smart things," the health secretary told a parliamentary inquiry this week. I doubt Silicon Valley would disagree. But the big tech companies might take issue with his next assertion: that it is their responsibility to stop teen sexting "because there is technology that can identify sexually explicit pictures and prevent [them] being transmitted".

Up to a point. Yes, there is software that can compare images against a database of explicit photographs and flag up matches. (This is used to limit the spread of child abuse pictures.) There is also software that can identify large enough swaths of skin tone in a picture to trigger a ban.

But these are blunt instruments, which can deliver false positives, and online censors have other issues. Facebook has struggled with some tough issues, facing criticism for banning some photographs. Those issues may be philosophical questions for the ages.

Next comes another social problem. Raging hormones, poor impulse control and an intuitive understanding of digital communications are a potent combination. If teenagers can't send a picture, they could upload it to a filesharing site and send their paramour the link. Or use a messaging service such as WhatsApp, which offers end-to-end encryption. Any regime that could outfox strategies like this would need to be intrusive, and would struggle to work in real-time.

At the same evidence session, Mr. Hunt also suggested that tech companies could identify cyberbullying through automated "word pattern recognition". Perhaps he knows something that the makers of Siri, Cortana and other personal assistants don't, because AIs struggle with the complexity of human conversation. Even humans misread snippets of text when they are divorced from tone, context and facial expression. Ask anyone who's had an argument on the Internet.

Mr. Hunt wants technological solutions to social problems. And no wonder — the National Health Service budget is under strain, and child mental health care resources are limited. The sexual health charity Brook cites research suggesting that 12% of 11 to 16-year-olds have seen or received sexual messages online, and when sexting goes wrong the consequences can be catastrophic. Some young people feel harassed and coerced into sending nudes. Others send a photo to one person, only to see it spread around their school. That can lead to bullying and even (rarely) suicide.

Most are unaware that they are committing a criminal offence. Some explicit pictures are classed as typical pornography, no matter the intention of the sender or age of the recipient.

Every parent would love to wave a magic tech wand and make problems like this disappear. The more immediate answer, however, is education. This week, the chairs of five select committees wrote to the government asking for sex and relationship education to be made compulsory in schools. Children would be taught about consent and coercion — how to say no, and how to respect others' right to say no. The government was unmoved.

That is a shame, because the striking thing about the iGeneration, as the academic Jean Twenge calls them, is how sober and strait-laced they are. A quarter of under-25s don't drink. Teenage pregnancies are at their lowest level since records began in 1969. The tech theorist Danah Boyd, who researched sexting among US teens, calls it "a very rational act with very irrational consequences". If we talk more about those consequences, it seems likely that young people will listen. And ultimately, finding a high-tech way to stop them sexting might be harder than convincing them it's a bad idea.

Total words: 758

Total Reading Time: _____ minutes _____ seconds

Vocabulary

pager *n.* 寻呼机
dictate *v.* 口述；指使；强行规定；支配
profanity *n.* 对神灵的亵渎；诅咒语
call centre *n.* 电话服务中心
steward *n.* （飞机、火车或船上的）乘务员；（大学、俱乐部等的）伙食管理员
wince *v.* （因痛苦或尴尬）龇牙咧嘴
parliamentary *adj.* 议会的

swath *n.* 一长条田地；一长条；一长片

blunt *adj.* 钝的，不锋利的；直言的

censor *n.* (书籍电影等的)审查员

raging *adj.* 强烈的；猛烈的；很严重的

hormone *n.* 荷尔蒙

encryption *n.* 加密；加密术

regime *n.* 政权；管理体制，政体

outfox *v.* 以智力胜过(或超过)

intrusive *adj.* 侵入的；烦扰的

session *n.* 一段时间，一场；(议会等的)会议，(法庭的)开庭

cyberbullying *n.* 网络欺凌

snippet *n.* 一小条(消息)；一则(新闻)

strain *n.* 紧张；重负，紧张；压力

harass *v.* 骚扰

coerce *v.* 强迫，胁迫；迫使

bullying *n.* 欺凌行为

pornography *n.* 淫秽作品

recipient *n.* 接受者，受方

wand *n.* 魔杖

coercion *n.* 强迫，胁迫

unmoved *adj.* 无动于衷的；冷漠的

sober *adj.* 清醒的；冷静的，素淡的

strait-laced *adj.* 拘谨保守的，古板的

irrational *adj.* 不合逻辑的；没有道理的

Phrases

flag up 使……注意；指出

be divorced from 与……离婚；脱离，与……分开

coerce ... into 强迫……做……

Notes

sexting: Sexting refers to sending, receiving, or forwarding sexually explicit messages, photographs, or videos, primarily between mobile phones, of oneself to others. It may also include the use of a computer or any other digital device.

Silicon Valley: Silicon Valley is a region in Northern California that serves as a global center for high technology and innovation.

WhatsApp: WhatsApp, or WhatsApp Messenger, is an American freeware, cross-platform centralized instant messaging (IM) and voice-over-IP (VoIP) service owned by Meta Platforms. It allows users to send text messages and voice messages, make voice and video calls, and share images, documents, user locations, and other content.

Exercises

I. Answer the following questions after reading the text.

1. What does the social problem mainly refer to in the text?

2. What does "blunt instruments" mean in paragraph 5?

3. What consequences might sexting result in for teenagers?

4. What were the government's attitudes towards the sex and relationship education?

5. From the writer's perspective, how can the social problems like sexting be solved more immediately and easily?

II. Decide whether the following statements are true or false according to the text.

1. The writer held that the big tech companies would frown upon the statements of the health secretary.

2. From the text we can learned that the technology industry can totally stop teen sexting from being transmitted.

3. Mr. Hunt resorts to technology to cope with social problems and finds it feasible.

4. In fact, many senders don't know that they are committing a criminal offence when sending some pornography pictures.

5. According to the text, the government is rather concerned about the sex and relationship education and will take some effective actions.

III. Fill in the blanks with the words given in the brackets. Change the form where necessary.

1. This problem raises the suspicion that such work resulted from a process of _____ (dictate) and transcription.

2. The girl _____ (wince) in pain from the stitches in her back when she reached down to the floor.

3. It is very easy to understand the reason _____ (parliamentary) adopted the approach that it did.

4. No matter how neutral his face was at that moment, the man's eyes burned with an almost uncontrollable _____ (raging).

5. And, now 70, the old man has turned out for the club ever since, _____ (outfox) many a batsman with those slow left-handers.

6. And I really must apologize to Jayden for _____ (intrusive) on his evening ...

although, it did make for some interesting explanations later on.

7. On many occasions, children may be reluctant to admit to being the victims of _____ (cyberbullying).

8. What is the impact of stresses and _____ (strain) from external forces on our practice field?

9. I was never _____ (coerce) or forced into doing anything I didn't like.

10. It seems to me that philosophers are often criticized for always demanding _____ (irrational) explanations.

IV. Translate the following sentences into Chinese.

1. One of my friends had a pager, and to reach her you had to phone an operator and dictate a message.

2. But the big tech companies might take issue with his next assertion: that it is their responsibility to stop teen sexting "because there is technology that can identify sexually explicit pictures and prevent [them] being transmitted."

3. Most are unaware that they are committing a criminal offence. Some explicit pictures are classed as typical pornography, no matter the intention of the sender or age of the recipient.

4. Children would be taught about consent and coercion — how to say no, and how to respect others' right to say no.

5. And ultimately, finding a high-tech way to stop them sexting might be harder than convincing them it's a bad idea.

V. Topics for discussion.

1. In your opinion, what age it's appropriate for children to use a smartphone?

2. Can you give some suggestions on how to prevent teens visiting bad websites?

References

［1］陈羽纶.美英报刊科技文章选读［M］.北京：北京大学出版社,1997.

［2］陈则航.英语阅读教学与研究［M］.北京：外语教学与研究出版社,2016.

［3］端木义万.美英报刊阅读教程（高级精选本）［M］.北京：北京大学出版社,2001.

［4］傅伟良.英文经济报刊文章选读［M］.北京：中国人民大学出版社,2009.

［5］黄远振.英语阅读教学与思维发展［M］.南宁：广西教育出版社,2019.

［6］卫春艳,康慧,吉哲民.美英报刊阅读理论与实践［M］.北京：国防工业出版社,2012.

［7］王笃勤.英语阅读教学［M］.北京：外语教学与研究出版社,2012.

［8］周学艺.美英报刊文章选读（上）［M］.北京：清华大学出版社,1997.

［9］周学艺.美英报刊文章选读（下）［M］.北京：清华大学出版社,2005.

［10］Interconnected Economy: Is Your Business At Risk?[EB/OL]. (2021−09−22)[2021−09−28]. https: //www.forbes.com/sites/sap/2021/09/22/interconnected-economy-is-your-business-at-risk/?sh=36a02be55467.

［11］Collaboration Overload Is Sinking Productivity[EB/OL]. (2021−09−07)[2021−10−06]. https: //hbr.org/2021/09/collaboration-overload-is-sinking-productivity.

［12］The Secret Behind Successful Corporate Transformations[EB/OL]. (2021−09−14)[2021−10−10]. https: //hbr.org/2021/09/the-secret-behind-successful-corporate-transformations?ab=hero-main-text.

［13］Why It's Harder to Change Culture than Nature[EB/OL]. (2021−03−07)[2021−10−16]. https: //www.latimes.com/opinion/story/2021−03−07/culture-wars-science-covid-pandemic.

［14］Cancel Culture Has Dababy Gone Too Far[EB/OL]. (2021−09−03)[2021−10−18]. http: //www.vsuspectator.com/2021/09/03/cancel-culture-has-dababy-gone-too-far/.

［15］Why Art and Culture Is Good for the Soul, the West End and the UK[EB/OL]. (2021−06−21)[2021−10−19]. https://www.standard.co.uk/culture/artoflondon/art-culture-west-end-uk-b940786.html.

［16］How Texting Could Improve Your Health[EB/OL]. (2020−11−03)[2021−10−21]. https://www.readersdigest.co.uk/health/wellbeing/how-texting-could-improve-your-health.

［17］How to Deal with Stress (there are plenty of ways!)[EB/OL]. [2021−10−22]. https://www.readersdigest.co.uk/health/health-conditions/how-to-deal-with-stress-there-are-plenty-of-ways.

［18］Do You Have Social Jet Lag? Here's What to Do[EB/OL]. (2021−08−12)[2021−10−25]. https: //edition.cnn.com/2021/08/12/health/irregular-sleep-social-jet-lag-wellness/index.html.

[19] A History of Wedding Dresses[EB/OL]. (2021−06−02)[2021−10−15]. https: //www. readersdigest.co.uk/lifestyle/fashion-beauty/a-history-of-wedding-dresses.

[20] Getting a Haircut Can Boost Your Mental Health[EB/OL]. [2021−10−28]. https: //www. readersdigest.co.uk/lifestyle/fashion-beauty/getting-a-haircut-can-boost-your-mental-health.

[21] The Evolution of Makeup[EB/OL]. (2020−11−30)[2021−10−30]. https: //www.readersdigest. co.uk/lifestyle/fashion-beauty/the-evolution-of-makeup.

[22] Going Deep Into Oyster Country[EB/OL]. (2021−12−03)[2021−12−05]. https: //www.nytimes. com/2021/12/03/travel/oysters-maryland-virginia-african-american-history.html.

[23] Fergus Henderson's "Whole Animal" Recipes Inspired Chefs on Both Sides of the Atlantic[EB/ OL]. (2021−02−28)[2021−10−08]. https: //www.theguardian.com/food/2021/feb/28/jay-rayner-on-restaurants-fergus-hendersons-inspirational-whole-animal-eating.

[24] Angkor: Asia's ancient "Hydraulic City"[EB/OL]. (2021−12−03)[2021−12−10]. https: //www. bbc.com/travel/article/20211201-angkor-asias-ancient-hydraulic-city.

[25] The Scottish Isle Where Native Ponies Roam[EB/OL]. (2021−12−01)[2021−12−13]. https: // www.bbc.com/travel/article/20211129-the-scottish-isle-where-native-ponies-roam.

[26] The Secret to a Fight-Free Relationship[EB/OL]. (2021−09−13)[2021−11−06]. https: //www. theatlantic.com/family/archive/2021/09/delaying-conflict-better-venting-relationships-scheduled-disagreement/620057/.

[27] If Bill and Melinda Gates Can't Make a Marriage Work, What Hope Is There for the Rest of Us?[EB/OL]. (2021−05−04)[2021−11−15]. https: //www.washingtonpost.com/ lifestyle/2021/05/04/gates-divorce-bill-melinda-marriage/.

[28] In Defense of Our Teachers[EB/OL]. (2020−07−21)[2021−12−18]. https: //www. theatlantic.com/culture/archive/2020/07/dave-grohl-pandemic-reopening-schools-health-teachers/614422/.

[29] Choosing Between Housing on or off Campus[EB/OL]. (2021−12−02)[2021−12−22]. https: // www.usnews.com/education/best-colleges/paying-for-college/articles/what-to-know-about-choosing-between-housing-on-or-off-campus.

[30] The Big Decisions that Impact Your Career[EB/OL]. (2021−05−31)[2021−09−05]. https: //hbr. org/2021/05/the-big-decisions-that-impact-your-career.

[31] Why You Should Build a "Career Portfolio"(Not a "Career Path")[EB/OL]. (2021−10−13) [2021−11−25]. https: //hbr.org/2021/10/why-you-should-build-a-career-portfolio-not-a-career-path.

[32] Reshaping Your Career in the Wake of the Pandemic[EB/OL]. (2021−04−21) [2021−09−09]. https: //hbr.org/2021/04/reshaping-your-career-in-the-wake-of-the-pandemic?registration=success.

[33] The Art Exploring the Truth About How Climate Change Began[EB/OL]. (2021−10−20) [2021−12−13]. https: //www.bbc.com/culture/article/20211020-the-art-exploring-the-truth-about-how-climate-change-began.

[34] Can Stand-up Comedy Help Mental Health?[EB/OL]. (2020−11−06)[2021−10−07]. https: //

www.readersdigest.co.uk/inspire/humour/can-stand-up-comedy-help-mental-health.

［35］ Comedy Is in Crisis, No Joke — But Venues and Comics Are Finding Ways to Fight Back[EB/OL].(2021-02-11)[2021-10-11]. https: //www.standard.co.uk/culture/comedy/comedy-crisis-venues-comedians-fight-back-covid-lockdown-b919094.html.

［36］ What is Medina Spirit's Legacy Following His Sudden Death? The Answer Is Uncertain[EB/OL].(2021-10-18). https: //www.latimes.com/sports/story/2021-12-07/medina-spirit-sudden-death-legacy-unclear-kentucky-derby-possible-disqualification.

［37］ Modern Sports Psychology and How It's Changed Sport in the UK[EB/OL]. [2021-10-26]. https: //www.readersdigest.co.uk/health/wellbeing/modern-sports-psychology-and-how-its-changed-sport-in-the-uk.

［38］ Powerlifter Karenjeet Kaur Bains Wants to Inspire More Women to Take up Strength Sports[EB/OL]. (2021-12-07)[2021-12-10]. https: //us.cnn.com/2021/12/07/sport/karenjeet-kaur-bains-powerlifting-cmd-spt-intl/index.html.

［39］ Effort to Reframe Climate Change as a Health Crisis Gains Steam[EB/OL]. (2021-11-04)[2021-11-06]. https: //www.nytimes.com/2021/11/04/climate/public-health-climate-change.html

［40］ Facebook Is Changing Its Name To Meta as It Focuses on the Virtual World[EB/OL]. (2021-10-28) [2021-10-30]. https: //www.washingtonpost.com/technology/2021/10/28/facebook-meta-name-change.

［41］ It's Time to Shift from the "War on Terror" to a War on Climate Change[EB/OL]. (2021-11-07) [2021-11-08]. https: //www.theguardian.com/commentisfree/2021/nov/07/its-time-to-shift-from-the-war-on-terror-to-a-war-on-climate-change.

［42］ Rebranding as Meta, Facebook Emphasizes VR Future over Crisis-beset Present[EB/OL]. (2021-10-28) [2021-10-30]. https: //www.latimes.com/business/technology/story/2021-10-28/facebook-changes-name-to-meta-signaling-emphasis-on-virtual-reality.

［43］ The Metaverse Is Coming and It's a Very Big Deal[EB/OL]. (2020-07-05)[2021-10-30]. https: //www.forbes.com/sites/cathyhackl/2020/07/05/the-metaverse-is-coming--its-a-very-big-deal/?sh=679b04bb440f.

［44］ Young Climate Activists Warn Their Elders: Stop Destroying the Planet[EB/OL]. (2021-11-04) [2021-11-06]. https: //www.latimes.com/world-nation/story/2021-11-04/first-youth-generation-to-experience-acute-climate-crisis-are-invigorated.

［45］ How Western Society Has Commercialised Yoga[EB/OL]. (2021-03-02)[2021-10-28]. https: //www.readersdigest.co.uk/inspire/life/how-western-society-has-commercialised-yoga.

［46］ Why we should normalize divorce talk[EB/OL]. [2021-10-30]. https: //www.readersdigest.co.uk/lifestyle/dating-relationships/why-we-should-normalize-divorce-talk.

［47］ Sometimes Talking, Not Tech, Is the Answer to Social Problems[EB/OL]. (2016-12-03) [2021-11-09]. https: //www.ft.com/content/a2dc898e-b895-11e6-961e-a1acd97f622d.